THE PATH THROUGH THE CIRCLE OF TIME

THE LIGHTBRINGER TRILOGY

THE QUEST FOR THE SWORD OF INFINITY

THE LAND WHERE SERPENTS RULE

THE PATH THROUGH THE CIRCLE OF TIME

THE PATH THROUGH THE CIRCLE OF TIME

Samantha Lee

WITH ILLUSTRATIONS BY
PAT HANNAH

Arlington Books
Clifford Street Mayfair
London

THE PATH THROUGH
THE CIRCLE OF TIME
first published 1980 by
Arlington Books (Publishers) Ltd
3 Clifford Street Mayfair
London W1

Set in England by
Inforum Ltd Portsmouth
Printed by A. Wheaton & Co Ltd
Exeter, Devon
Bound by Biddles Ltd
King's Lynn, Norfolk

British Library Cataloguing in Publication Data
Lee, Samantha
The path through the circle of time.
823' .9 1J PZ7 .L/
ISBN 0-85140-508-8

To Stevie, my golden son

Contents

Prologue

In the unrecorded days of the distant past, the Sun-Kings ruled the world.

A dynasty of golden beings, born of the Sun, they held sway over the elements. Earth, Air, Fire and Water were theirs to command. But though wise in all other things, they never learned the secret of Immortality.

And so, after tens of thousands of years had passed, Zoltan, last of the great Sun-Kings, died. And with his death the light faded from the golden age of Man.

Zoltan left one son, a Semi-Mortal born of a human mother. His name was Owen Lightbringer. He rose from the ashes of the dying dynasty to claim the legendary Sword of Infinity — "forged by unknown forces, aeons before Time began, to last a million years beyond Eternity."

His quest for the magic weapon led Owen and his Bond-Servant, the Wolfeslayer, through many perilous adventures. Together they faced the vicious Hawkheads, battled against the Semi-Human Troogs, and grappled with the fearful Marshe-Wraithes of the Forest of Mists.

And all the while, Zathranax, Black Magus of the Infinities, monitored their every step. On a magic crystal eye which hung in the throne room of his mountain eyrie, Castle Karnage, the dread Dragon Lord and his hunch-backed henchman, the snivelling Strang, watched the progress of the Son of the Sun with avid interest.

For Zathranax was the sworn enemy of the Sun dynasty and his insane desire for world domination was only surpassed by his insatiable ambition to secure the Sword of Infinity for himself.

At Owen's investiture in the great temple of Stonehenge, Xanthos, Warrior Priest of the Sun, had presented the Lightbringer with two invaluable assets: the All-Seeing Ring, in the depths of whose dark blue stone lay the accumulated knowledge of the Sun Dynasty, and the Staff of Strength, an ancient piece of wood reputedly carved from the first living tree. Without these, Owen might never have reached his destination — the mysterious Pyramid of Anakrion, within whose walls dwelt the Ancient King. With them, and the help of Big Donal and Tagon of the Trees, he was able to gain his Sword and defeat the Dragon Lord's wicked plans.

Yet an even harder challenge now faced the Lightbringer. To ensure the future of the Sun Dynasty he must marry the only surviving female of the line, the Princess Aneira, Fairest of the Fair.

But Aneira lay in a serum-induced sleep in the Land where Serpents ruled. The way to this fearful place lay through the Waters of Oblivion, a treacherous stretch of the seas from which no man had ever been known to return . . . alive.

On their voyage, Owen and Wolfe faced mutiny from the one-eyed Captain Darkangel and his villainous crew, and terror in the many and varied shapes of Arathusa, Queen of the Deeps.

Had it not been for the able assistance of Delmo, the talking Dolphin and his friend Narwol, the Sealman, the Lightbringer might never have survived his encounter with that dread lady and come at last safely to the Land of Serpents.

Prologue

There, Aneira, Princess of Light, lay captive of the poisonous Snake-People, in the huge temple which dominated the Tiered City.

The Temple of Axylotan, wherein dwelt the seven-headed Serpent God, guarded by a hideous army of invincible Zombies known as the Twice-Born. These living dead were all that remained of the human sacrifices offered up to Axylotan by the evil High Priest of the Snake Cult, Ssalazar. Revived in the Venom Tanks, in the depths of the great Temple, the Twice-Born could not be killed . . . for they were already dead. Against them even the mighty Sword of Infinity was to prove powerless. But in the old saying "It takes a Twice-Born to kill a Twice-Born twice," was found the seed of their destruction.

During the course of this monumental struggle, Wolfe slew Ssalazar, and presented the Son of the Sun with yet another problem.

To awaken Aneira from her drugged sleep, Owen must place upon her finger the Magic Iron Ring of Tara. Only Ssalazar knew the whereabouts of this mysterious country. And he took the secret with him to his watery grave.

All would have been lost but for the power of yet another Ring, the All-Seeing Ring of the Sun-Kings. With it, Owen reached beyond death to glean the information he needed to set him on the road to Tara . . .

ONE

The Boatman

Mawg crouched by the water's edge, the long, bone needle moving deftly in his hand. In. Out. In. Out. The thong snapped like a whiplash as it bit into the leather hides that covered the wooden frame of the small, round boat. He stretched the last corner of the patch taut, fastening off the binding with a series of complicated overstitches, then severed the end with a sharpened flint. He covered the whole repair with boiling pitch scooped from a dented pot that rested on the smouldering embers of the peat fire. The mixture cooled rapidly in the freezing northern air, setting rock hard.

He stood up, smoothing the stiffness from his cramped knee joints and contemplated his handiwork with grim satisfaction.

"Good as new," he muttered, wiping a drop of moisture from his reddened nose with the soiled cuff of his woollen overshirt. "Good as new," and he patted the crude painting that decorated the coracle's blackened hull. It showed a winged serpent and beside it that universal eye, which keeps watch on the fortunes of all sailors, from the Outer Reaches to the Isles of the Blessed.

There was a sudden crackling in the undergrowth that

fringed the shoreline, and Mawg swung round, clutching instinctively at the Narwal's tooth that hung on a plaited fibre cord around his scraggy neck. It had been carved in the shape of a severed head, a charm with powerful magic in it.

Two men emerged from the waist-high bracken that bordered the scrubby sand-dunes.

The first, a tall, handsome youth of about twenty summers, wore his thick, flaxen hair low on his forehead, bound with a filet of beaten gold decorated with a single tiger-eye stone. Over his light chainmail vest and leggings and his pale leather thigh-boots was thrown an all-enveloping cloak of dark brown wool lined with reynard fur. A sudden gust of wind flipped the heavy garment away from his body. Mawg noted, with a sinking feeling in the pit of his stomach, the huge sword that hung in the jewelled scabbard around his waist.

The youth's companion was less spectacular. A man of

middle years and medium height, thickset, with close-cropped hair that matched the grizzled stubble coating the square line of his jaw. His cloak, over serviceable woollen tunic and breeches, was grey and unadorned.

He it was who spoke first.

"Well, well, well! And what have we here? A man or a monkey?"

For Mawg, who stood only waist high to the shortest of the two strangers, did indeed bear an unfortunate resemblance to an ape. His hunched body and low simian forehead had been beaten black by the harsh weather of the inaptly-named Isles of the Blessed, and his wide, slack mouth, pulled back now at the corners in a grimace of fear, made him appear more animal than human.

The people of the Outer Isles were a taller, fairer breed, but those on the central islands of Coom and Kilken, the last relics of the ancient race that had once populated the whole area, held fast to their old, dark religion. They were known as the 'little people', and they guarded jealously this, their last stronghold, against 'the interlopers' who had stolen their other lands. Such was the reputation of the Inner Isles, that few strangers ever set foot on them.

"Don't you touch me," gibbered Mawg, his voice tinged with the courage of desperation. "I have a sister who has the evil eye. Don't come any nearer or I'll not be responsible for the consequences."

The thickset man roared with laughter.

"Will you not?" he guffawed. "Then I'd better mind my manners."

"Just so," said the younger man. "There are times, Wolfe, when your manners leave a lot to be desired. I'm ashamed of you, speaking to this gentleman in such a fashion."

He knelt beside Mawg and stared into the little man's close-set, black eyes.

"Do not be afraid," he said gently. "We mean you no harm."

But Mawg was far from reassured. In fact, what he saw was enough to make him leap into his boat and paddle away for dear life, except that his legs seemed suddenly to have become rooted in the shingle.

For the eyes that looked into his were not human eyes at all. They were gold-flecked and almond-shaped with the elongated irises of a great hunting cat.

"Who . . . who . . . who are you?" stammed Mawg. "What . . . what do you want?"

"My name is Owen Lightbringer," said the lynx-eyed stranger. "And this is my friend, the Wolfeslayer."

"And whom do we have the pleasure of addressing?" enquired the latter, with a mock bow.

"They . . . they call me M–M–Mawg." The little man's voice was coloured by a strong, lilting brogue.

"Well, Mawg," said Owen Lightbringer. "Perhaps you can help us? We are looking for the Long Barrow of Kilken."

The skin on Mawg's forearms crumpled into gooseflesh.

"Now what would you be wantin' with that cursed place?" he quavered.

"That's our business," growled Wolfe. "Do you know where it is or don't you?"

"Of course I know where it is," said Mawg. "It's over the water. But I'd not recommend you go there. It's hardly a place for sightseeing."

The young man gave a muffled exclamation of displeasure.

"Over the water?" he said, pulling his cloak around him to ward off the piercing cold. "Then we've miscalculated our landing? We're not on Kilken?"

"Indeed not. You'd not find anybody on Kilken. Anybody living that is. This is Coom. Kilken is over Westaways."

"It's this blasted fog," complained the Wolfeslayer, blow-

ing on his frostbitten hands. "That's what confused us. The cursed stuff is getting thicker all the time."

And, indeed, the sea-mist that had been hovering over the dull, grey water had begun to curl inwards towards the land as what little wind there was dropped with the approach of night.

Mawg looked slyly from one man to another. It was evident now that they weren't going to murder him out of hand. He touched the severed head at his collar-bone in a gesture of silent thanks. His confidence began to creep back and with it the blood to his paralysed limbs. He even sniffed a chance of profit. A chance that came seldom enough on the island of Coom.

He cleared his throat.

"I . . . I . . . could take you if you like," he gulped. "To Kilken."

"In this fog?" scoffed Wolfe. "You jest, little man."

"Sure this is nothing." Mawg was scorn itself. "I've sailed in fogs fifty times worse than this. Fogs where you couldn't see your hand in front of you."

"But how will you take bearings?" asked Owen.

"Bearings?" The little man was clearly confused.

"How will you plot your course? If you cannot see the stars? How will you find landfall?"

"The stars?" cackled Mawg. "And what would I be needing with the stars? Sure they're fine things to keep a man company on a bright night. But the bright nights on the Isles of the Blessed are few and far between. I'd be in a right state if I was depending on the stars to show me the way. I've been sailing these waters since I was knee-high to a grasshopper, and my father sailed them before me, and his father before him, but never a one of us sailed by the stars."

"How then?"

"Why, by the feel of the current bending beneath the boat,

by the water warming as it reaches out to the land, and by other signs which cannot be learnt, only felt. I feel them," said the little man simply. "And I say I can take you to Kilken — if you're daft enough to want to go."

There was silence as he finished speaking. The grey fog crept in over the grey stones. Somewhere out in the shrouded bay, a lone seal barked.

At last Wolfe spoke.

"What do you think, Owen?"

"I think we were lucky to have chanced upon Mawg. If he is willing to take us, then I am willing to go."

"You'll pay of course," said the Boatman hastily, before the stranger had a chance to change his mind.

"Of course. You shall have two deenars when you put us down on Kilken."

"Two deenars?" Mawg's jaw dropped. "Sure, you must be made of money . . . But wait a while now," he added suspiciously. "What's to stop you from leaving me without payment when I get you there? I'd better be having the money in advance."

"Are you suggesting . . ." began the Wolfeslayer furiously, but the young man placed a restraining hand on his arm.

"Let's compromise," he said. "One deenar now. One when we get there."

"Done," said the little man, spitting on his hand and holding it out to seal the bargain.

Without removing the jewelled gauntlet that covered his right hand, Owen Lightbringer reached for Mawg's grubby fist. Over the glove, on his index finger, he wore a silver ring of strange design, in which sat a dark blue stone.

As the two hands came in contact, Mawg felt a peculiar sensation run up his arm, as though a current of energy was passing from the stranger's body into his. He let go abruptly, massaging the palm to get rid of the odd, tingling sensation.

What had he let himself in for? A trip to the Island of the Dead with two . . . two what? Still, two deenars was not to be sniffed at. It was as much as he would see in a year at the fishing. And the fishing had been bad lately.

He took the proferred gold coin, bit it experimentally, then, noticing the look of displeasure in the Wolfeslayer's eyes, tucked it hastily into the woven pouch at his waist.

"You'd better get in the boat," he said, committing himself once and for all.

"Will it hold three?" asked the Wolfeslayer dubiously. "It looks a bit flimsy to me. I don't fancy drowning in this weather."

"Hold three?" snorted Mawg. "Haven't I had six bullocks in her before now? Hop in I said, or we'll miss the tide."

He held the cockleshell craft steady while first the tall, fair youth and then his grumbling companion, clambered aboard.

When they were settled, he leapt in smartly himself and, pushing the boat away from the shingle with a roughly-fashioned oar, began to skull rapidly into the mist-hidden waters of the bay.

"I should get some sleep if I were you," he advised. "We'll hardly be there before sunrise."

TWO

The Long Barrow of Kilken

Owen and Wolfe stirred in the damp morning air, stretching their cramped limbs and yawning fitfully.

Before them, rising from the sea like a whale's humped back, stood the stark outline of Kilken. A few gulls whirled, screeching, above the grey, rock cliffs. Otherwise there was no sign of life. The place had the dismal air of an abandoned burial ground.

Which is exactly what it was.

A huge graveyard. A place where for centuries the 'little people' had hurriedly buried their dead before fleeing back to the safety of the land of the living. A bleak slab of rock, set in the cold, northern sea, crowned by the biggest underground tomb ever fashioned by the hand of man. The Long Barrow of Kilken.

"There it is," shuddered Mawg. "Hurry up and get ready to jump off as soon as we touch land. This is not a place I'd like to be caught dead in while I'm still alive. And I'll be having my other deenar now if you don't mind."

He thrust his upturned palm under Owen's nose. The hand shook as though the little man had been overtaken by an attack of palsy.

"You fear Kilken greatly, do you not, Mawg?" observed

the Lightbringer.

"I do that," hissed the boatman. "It's an evil place. Sure, we all end up here — or somewhere like it — eventually, but isn't it best to put off the day as long as possible?"

The coracle's bottom grated on the shingle of the beach and Mawg's leathery face blanched white under his tan.

"Get out, get out!" he jabbered. "I've no wish to linger here."

"Keep your shirt on," said Wolfe heatedly. "I don't know what all the fuss is about."

"Well, you may know soon enough," muttered Mawg ominously. "And I'm not waiting to find out."

"Do you mean to tell me you've never actually been on Kilken, Mawg?" Owen was incredulous.

"I have not." The little man was obviously horrified at the very thought. "I've been this far, accompanying my father's corpse and . . ." Here he paused to touch the charm around his neck, ". . . and with my cousin Turley. But I've never set foot on the place. Only the Buryers do that. And if they want to take their life in their hands for gold, isn't it up to them?"

"Like you're doing now?" suggested Wolfe sarcastically.

"I am not," gibbered the boatman. "I've not left the coracle. And if you had any sense neither would you." He lowered his voice conspiratorially. "Nobody bides here . . . Nobody. And yet . . . it's only fair to warn you . . . while you have the chance to change your minds . . . there have been sightings . . . strange spirits . . . demons . . . creatures from another world . . ."

"Superstitious piffle," snorted Wolfe.

But Owen was looking thoughtful.

"Creatures from another world . . ." he mused. "I wonder . . . ?"

"Oh come on now, Owen," jibed Wolfe. "Don't tell me you believe this lunatic and his old wives' tales?"

"Don't dismiss them out of hand, Wolfe. You and I have seen some strange things on our travels. There might be something in it. These creatures. Couldn't they possibly come from the world we seek? From Tara?"

"Tara is it?" said Mawg. "Sure, everybody knows Tara doesn't exist. Only in the legends."

"We've been told different," Owen assured him. "We believe the entrance to it lies somewhere in the Long Barrow."

"The Gods preserve us," said Mawg in terror. "Surely you're not thinking of going in there to look?"

"Why not?"

"Nobody's been in that place for centuries. All the burials are done on the Plain of the Dead nowadays. It's bad enough your landing on the Island. But going into the Barrow. That's courting definite disaster."

"There's nothing else for it," said Wolfe brusquely. "We must go."

"Well, rather you than me," muttered Mawg. "Now, get out if you're going. One way or another I'm off. So make your minds up."

"Just a moment, Mawg," said Owen. "Before we go, I have a proposition for you."

"A what?"

"A bargain I'd like to strike with you, if you're willing."

"What kind of a bargain?"

"How would you like to make thirty deenars?"

Mawg's beady eyes popped open.

"Thirty deenars? Glory be! I didn't know there was that much money in the world. Thirty deenars! What would I have to do? Murder somebody?"

"Nothing so dramatic," grinned the Lightbringer. "All you have to do is come back every morning at this time for the next thirty days. For each day you come, you will earn one deenar — until the day we are here to meet you. On that day you will ferry us back to Coom and I will pay you the balance. What do you say?"

Mawg sniffed in disgust.

"What I say is, what if you never come back? I'll have had all my trouble for nothing."

"That's easily settled," said the young man, easing the blue-stoned ring from his gloved hand and placing it in the pocket of his vest. "I shall give you my gauntlet. If, by the end of thirty days, we have not returned, then you must take it to Xanthos, Warrior Priest of the Sun, at the Temple of Stonehenge. Tell him we are lost. Tell him of the bargain we made today. He will pay you your thirty deenars. And you shall have five now to cover your expenses on the journey."

"Have you taken leave of your senses, Owen?" Wolfe burst in. "Five deenars and your gauntlet? Why, the gauntlet itself is worth more than the thirty deenars you promised him. What's to stop him making off with both and leaving us here in the lurch?"

Mawg jumped guiltily. The same thought had just occurred to him.

"Why, there's nothing to stop him," agreed Owen. "But somehow I don't think he'll do that."

He pulled off the heavily embossed gauntlet and handed it to the boatman in silence.

Mawg's wide mouth dropped open and his eyes formed round O's of disbelief.

For the hand which held the glove towards him was like no other hand he had ever seen. It glowed in the clear morning sunlight, a bright, burning gold.

He took the gauntlet like a man in a trance.

"I am the Son of the Sun," explained the young man quietly. "And I need your help. Can I count on it? Are you to be trusted?"

Mawg squirmed uncomfortably under the direct, golden stare, thinking of the time he had filched the Narwal's tooth from Turley's corpse. It was one of the reasons he was so anxious to get clear of Kilken. At any moment he expected his cousin's shade to leap from behind a rock and accuse him of the theft. And speaking of theft, there was that piglet he had 'found' last week. His life until now had been far from blameless, even though his crimes had been petty ones. Did this young man know? Could he read minds as well as everything else? Mawg decided to take a chance.

"Of course I'm trustworthy," he blustered. "And I'll come every day . . . for thirty days . . . for you. Though I might not bother if it was your friend who was asking," he added spitefully.

"Very well, Mawg," smiled Owen. "I believe you. Here are your five deenars, and the one I owe you from our previous arrangment. Now, will you shake hands to seal our new bargain?"

Before he realised what he was doing, Mawg had placed his grubby paw in the young man's golden hand. Again he felt the strange current coursing through his body and suddenly, to his amazement, he realised that he was really going to stick to the bargain even though, moments before, he had no intention of doing any such thing.

He shook the hand away as though it were red hot and, pocketing the gold coins, took up his rough, wooden oars.

"For the last time, will you get out," he said gruffly. "If I don't go now I'll hardly be home before it's time to come back."

His two passengers disembarked at last and Mawg pushed his coracle away from the Island of the Dead with a heartfelt sigh of relief.

"Good luck," he muttered. "You'll need it."

But the two men didn't hear him. They were already heading for the shale hillface that rose steeply from the shallow beach.

They struggled up the treacherous slope.

"Two steps forward and three back," puffed Wolfe, as a small avalanche of pebbles slithered away under his feet.

"Not much further," Owen encouraged him. "There's grass up ahead."

And in a final burst of effort, they arrived breathlessly at the top.

They were on a flat plateau. As far as the eye could see, the sparse grass was dotted with small, granite cairns. Each pathetic pile of stones, heaped into a pyramid shape, marked the last resting place of a collection of bones that had once called itself a man.

Wolfe shivered, pulling his cloak around his stocky body and looking back the way he had come.

Out in the bay, Mawg manoeuvred the round boat expertly through the fingers of rock that stuck up like milestones in the grey-green water.

The sea looked cold and uninviting, but even so Wolfe found himself wishing he were back on the small bobbing craft. He turned to say as much to his companion, but Owen was already striding purposefully towards the series of hillocks that led to the centre of the Island and the Long Barrow.

Wolfe loped after him, catching him up at the bottom of the first rise. They climbed in silence, saving their breath for the long, upward haul. The ground beneath their feet was dangerously uneven, studded with sharp stones and outcroppings of moss, moist and slippery with morning dew.

Owen set a punishing pace. Anxious to get to their destination, he seemed not to be affected by the solitariness of the place. Wolfe, however, found himself continually looking over his shoulder — for what he did not know.

At last, panting with exertion, they topped the final rise.

Before them, crouching like a malevolent monster, lay the Long Barrow of Kilken, a festering sore on a pock-marked hillside. An air of suffocating desolation hung around the giant burial mound. No bird-song sounded here. The keening of the wind soughed around the great humped shape, like the voices of a thousand tormented souls crying out for release. But there was no way out for them. The entrance was sealed by an enormous basalt boulder, washed by the rain of ages into the shape of a bear's head. It stood, twice as high as a man, eyeing them balefully.

"Perhaps Mawg was right after all?" suggested the Wolfe-slayer, ashamed of his fears yet unable to dispel them. "Let's go back to the beach, Owen. I feel danger here as I've never felt it before."

"You go by all means," replied Owen, placing his golden hand on his companion's shoulder. "I, too, feel the evil and I would not lead you into danger unnecessarily. But I *must* go on. You know that. Without the Magic Ring of Tara, Aneira will never awaken. I will never have a son, the dynasty will die, and I will be condemned to living Hell for Eternity in the Pyramid of Anakrion. Whatever this tomb holds, it cannot be worse than that."

Wolfe sighed resignedly.

"Well," he said, "if you go, I go. Let's get on with it then before I change my mind."

"Good for you, Wolfe,' grinned Owen. "I knew you'd stick by me. Now, let's see if we can get in. Hold this for me, will you?" And he unclasped the heavy cloak and handed it to his friend.

Slowly and deliberately, as though gathering his energies for the ordeal to come, the Lightbringer rolled up his right sleeve. Like his hand, the arm, to the shoulder, glowed a burning gold. The muscles underneath the shining skin, rippled with latent power.

He slipped the thin gold band from his hair, handing it wordlessly to the Wolfeslayer, and shook the unruly flaxen mane away from his face.

In the centre of his forehead, a rayed disc, like a miniature sun, stood out like a golden tattoo.

The young man closed his eyes, face set in lines of concentration, and turned his forehead up towards the morning Sun.

As though drinking power from the round orange disc, the mark on his head began to pulse. Brighter and brighter it glowed until his whole face was suffused in an eerie light. Then, opening his eyes again, those strange, gold-flecked eyes with their elongated irises, he leant his golden shoulder against the great black rock, and began to push.

The giant boulder began to shudder, then to move, slowly, a hairsbreadth at a time, away from the entrance.

"Give me a hand, Wolfe," groaned the Sun-Prince, the

veins in his neck standing out with the effort.

Casting aside the cloak and hair ornament, Wolfe joined him, setting his broad back against the smooth surface of the stone and heaving for all he was worth.

And this last bit of pressure did the trick. With a sound like a tooth being pulled from its socket, the huge boulder rolled to one side.

In contrast to the rock that had guarded it, the entranceway was minute, a small square hole, built to admit one of Mawg's stature.

Without a backward glance, Owen bent down and crawled into the narrow opening.

Sweating with apprehension and effort, the Wolfeslayer struggled in after him.

The corridor that led from the doorway, was dank and smelled of stale air. But at least there was light. Guttering lamps, set at intervals into small niches in the slimy walls, gave off a feeble glow. Wolfe wondered nervously who, or what, kept the lamps lit.

As he passed the first of them he was horrified to notice that the lanterns were fashioned from human skulls, set in bowls of rancid oil in which coiled wicks floated like fat, grey worms. A stench of singeing hair, caught in his throat as he passed, making him gag. With his next step he felt something soft squirm under his boot. Its squeak, as it scuttled away in the darkness, mingled with Wolfe's involuntary exclamation of disgust.

"Wait for me, Owen!" he shouted, his voice close to panic.

But the Sun-Prince's retreating back was by now so far away as to be almost out of sight. His golden arm flashed in the lamplight as he turned to look back.

"Hurry, Wolfe!" he called, his voice echoing excitedly down the corridor. "There's some sort of chamber up ahead."

"I'm coming, I'm coming," grumbled Wolfe. "Whatever's

in there has waited this long for us. No doubt it'll wait a bit longer."

The tunnel was beginning to widen and, much to Wolfe's relief, the ceiling began to slope upwards. He was able to shuffle the last few steps in an almost upright position.

Owen was standing in the centre of what looked like a large, square chamber. It was difficult to judge the size as it was unlit, the only illumination coming from the skull-lamps that glowed fitfully from the corridor.

But there was no mistaking the function of the place. It reeked of the charnel-house.

As Wolfe stepped forward he tripped over a pile of human bones.

"Agador preserve us," he grunted. "What have we let ourselves in for this time?"

And as if in answer to his question, a slab of stone sliced downwards from the roof. It sealed the entrance to the tunnel and plunged them into total darkness.

Out of the darkness, a voice spoke.

"Ah, gentlemen," it said. "I've been expecting you."

THREE

The Tara Cards

A light flared in the darkness. It haloed a disembodied head, floating like a camellia in a sea of ink, and a skeletal hand which held aloft a taper.

The hand touched the taper to a tall, grey candle and the circle of light widened to reveal the body that grew from the head. It belonged to an old, old woman. She sat at a rickety table, on which lay an untidy pile of gaming cards.

"Come," said the old crone, gathering the cards into a dog-eared bundle. "Come. I will tell you your fortune."

And like obedient children, Owen and Wolfe crouched down before her.

With a deftness of hand that belied her age, the old woman began to shuffle the cards. Slightly larger than the normal play pack, they were bent at the edges and well-thumbed with use.

A wisp of hair detached itself from the unruly haystack that framed her sunken features. She paused to tuck the errant lock behind one wrinkled ear before laying the cards out, face downwards, in a circular pattern. When the circle was complete, she placed two more cards, side by side, in its centre, pushed the remainder of the pack to one side and looked up at the two men with eyes that shone unnaturally bright in the candle glow.

Too late, Owen became aware of the suffocating scent that rose from the yellow vapours of the candle-flame. Too late, he appreciated the simplicity of the ruse that had captured his attention while the mesmeric drugs did their work. His senses had already been dulled to the point where he was aware of only two things in the darkened chamber. The eyes of the woman and the pack of cards that lay face downwards on the blue baize tabletop.

He knew that Wolfe, beside him, would be similarly enthralled.

"Look closely," commanded the old woman.

The cards danced before Owen's eyes like animated pennants.

"These are the Tara cards," continued the ancient. "They foretell what is yet to come. All that will befall should you enter the forbidden world of Tara. There is still a chance for you to change your mind. As I speak, Time is frozen, but should I turn the first card, then the wheels of future events will be put into motion. There will be no escape. The choice is yours. Well, Semi-Mortal, what shall I do? Shall I turn the card . . . or not?"

Owen's head felt like a pumpkin full of straw. The woman's words echoed in his mind in separate segments, jumbled as a jigsaw puzzle. He struggled to piece them together, to make sense of her questions.

"What is the alternative?" he asked finally, his voice sounding clumsily in his ears, as though his tongue had swollen across his throat to block the escaping words.

The ancient gave a sharp cackle of laughter. With a dusty slipper, she nudged one of the many mounds of bones that littered the floor. The pile collapsed. The sound, as it clattered down, magnified in Owen's disorientated brain to almost deafen him.

"There is your alternative," she sniggered. "The way you came is sealed. You cannot go back. You must go on. Or stay here . . . and rot."

"You leave us little choice," mumbled Owen.

"There are some things worse than death, Semi-Mortal," warned the old woman.

"I will take that chance."

"And you . . . *Twice Born?"

The crone turned her bird-bright gaze on the Wolfeslayer. The stubble stood out lividly against his pallid cheeks as he struggled to answer her from the numbness that crept

* Wolfe was a Twice-Born due to the dangerously magical powers of Arathusa, Queen of the Deeps, who had brought him back from the dead for her own evil pleasure during his adventures with Owen when they had sought the Land of the Serpents. The Twice-Born, although they feel pain, are indestructible — as Wolfe had learnt to his advantage on a number of occasions.

through his brain.

"Where Owen goes . . ." he forced through clenched teeth. "I go."

"Then it is settled," chortled the Fortune-teller. "We can proceed."

The first card she turned was the one which lay on the right hand side, in the centre of the circle. On it, a great rayed sun, ablaze in an ochre sky, shone down on an orange field in which a small golden child sat playing with a yellow ball.

"The Sun," said the old woman. "That represents you, Semi-Mortal."

Owen stared at the card. The smell of the incense was almost overpowering. The huge Sun swam before his eyes like a mirage in the desert.

The decrepit figure turned over the sister card of the central pair, then pointed accusingly at the Wolfeslayer.

"And that is you, Twice-Born," she hooted. "The Fool. For that is what you are. You stand to gain nothing from this journey, yet you put yourself in danger in the name of friendship."

The person that confronted Wolfe wore the traditional cap and bells. Over his shoulder was slung a cloth bag and in one hand he carried a wilting flower. A tiny dog yapped at his heels but the figure had eyes for nothing but the brightly-coloured butterfly that hovered above him. So engrossed was he in this beautiful, transient vision, he failed to see the cliff that fell away beneath his feet.

The old woman turned her attention to the cards in the circle. She flipped them over one at a time, keeping up a continuous commentary as each tiny world within a world was revealed.

The first showed a man, dressed in red, a green halo flaring from his streaming hair. He hung, upside down, anchored by one foot to the outstretched branch of a giant oak-tree.

"The hanged man," chuckled the old woman. "He will present you with a problem of such dimension that it will negate your trip to Tara. For in resolving your present problem you will create an even greater one for another who is yet to come."

The card that followed was stark and simple. A great black sword on a background of blood.

"Death," announced the crone, with drooling satisfaction. "It stalks you in many forms. "I see a hound with eyes of coal, a creature from the depths, half-man, half-beast, a fiend from the inner regions of your own conscience. . . ."

Eagerly she moved on.

A man with wild hair and a flowing red cloak looked out from behind a table on which stood an assortment of objects. A coin. A sword. A cup. A club. In his left hand he brandished an iron wand.

"The Magician. Giobnhu. Iron-Smith of Tara. He who forged the Magic Ring you seek. A good friend . . . or a dire enemy. "The Temptress." A voluptuous woman, her coiled, auburn tresses threaded with ivy, sat framed against a dark green sky. By her side, a cornucopia filled to overflowing with exotic fruits. In her right hand, an ear of corn.

"Universal Mother. Harbinger of Life . . . and Death," droned the old woman. "Ruler of the Palace of Dreams. In her hands lies your future. And here . . . the Chariot."

The young man who stood, proud and erect, in the fiery carriage filled Owen with a strange sense of unease. He was golden, as a Sun-King, yet his hair shone like fire from the printed page.

"All this has happened before," thought the Lightbringer. "Or will happen again. Or both. I know this man but I have never seen him. Or have I?"

But his confused speculations were brought to an end by the hag turning up another picture.

Owen caught his breath.

The girl who knelt by the stream, her silver body uncovered save for the sparkling waterfall of hair that fell to her waist, was the most beautiful creature he had ever seen. More beautiful that his long-lost Mother, Dorelia, for whom the Sun-King, Zoltan, had died of love. More beautiful even than his betrothed Aneira, Fairest of the Fair. Behind her shining head, a million sparkling planets winked in the purple firmament.

"The Star-Child," said the old one. "Heiress to the Universe, Ward of the Temptress Danu, Promised of Cernunnos, the Horned-One."

Card number seven was made up of the three figures from the three previous cards. On it the young man held the Star-Child close to him while the Temptress, her expression betraying deadly fury, looked on.

"What's this?" asked the old woman, hurriedly turning the next card. "There must be some mistake."

The face that leapt out at them was evil personified. The slit eyes were laden with malice and the thin lips drawn back from the pointed teeth in a feral snarl. The body above the waist was that of a man. Below, the haunches of a goat tapered into cloven hooves. From the shoulderblades sprouted a pair of leathery wings and the long, bearded head was topped by a huge set of branching antlers. A stout chain, threaded through a ring in the base of the column on which this monster crouched, held captive two pathetically small figures. A golden boy and a girl with silvery hair.

"Ah, Cernunnos," the ancient nodded her satisfaction. "Then all is well."

She flipped the penultimate card, then stared at it in disbelief, It was identical to the one she had first turned over. The Sun. Only this time it lay upside down. The old woman's grey face turned several shades greyer. Hastily she scooped up the cards, shuffled them and laid them out in the original pattern. One by one she turned them up. They had fallen precisely as before.

The Sun. The Fool. The Hanged Man. Death. The Magician. The Temptress. The Chariot. The Star-Child. The Lovers. The Horned God . . . and again the Sun . . . upside down.

"What can it mean?" muttered the old woman, wiping the sweat from her raddled features.

"Why?" Owen's voice sounded from far, far away. "What's the matter?"

"What can it mean?" repeated the old woman. "Can't you see? Don't you realise? There is only *one* Sun in the Tara pack."

With trembling hands she turned over the last card. It showed a great wheel of light, revolving in a sea of stars. Through its centre a jagged path ran like a scarlet wound. The old hag gave a wail of pure terror.

"The Circle of Time," she moaned. "There is a break in the Circle of Time!"

The shining ellipse revolved under Owen's gaze until he felt sick and giddy. He shut his eyes to ward off the sensation. But even through closed lids it pursued him, growing in size until the swirling light filled his head.

A rending, groaning sound, as though the world were being torn apart, forced him to open his eyes. As he did so, the old woman, her table and the pack of cards disappeared, blown away by the gust of wind that extinguished the candle-flame.

And Owen felt himself falling. Falling into a pitch black well of darkness. Instinctively he reached out to where the Wolfeslayer had been moments before. But his hand clutched only emptiness.

He tumbled over and over in the void. Lights flashed before his eyes, kaleidoscopic colours far outside the spectrum of human vision. Noises battered his eardrums, a cacophany which covered the whole range of sound from the deepest groan to the shrillest shriek. Strange tastes coated his tongue. Diverse smells, sweet and loathesome, filled his nostrils. He felt velvet under his hands, while thorns pricked his skin and cool cloths soothed his fevered forehead.

Fear and delight, apprehension and despair, love and hate, all the sensations of life rolled over and around him in one gigantic assault on the senses.

Finally, when he could endure no more, the blackness that engulfed his body flooded into his battered brain and he lost consciousness.

FOUR

The Valley Obscured by Trees

Owen came to in a wooded valley surrounded by hills. The Wolfeslayer's prone body lay, like a crumpled rag, beside him.

They were in a small clearing, carpeted by orange moss and hemmed in by trees. Purple trees. Each leaf, branch and trunk glowed the same searing colour. Above them a dark violet sun hung panting in a burnt ochre sky.

Owen sat up and tested his limbs for breakages. His body felt like one enormous bruise but all his bones seemed to be intact. His head throbbed painfully in the sun's violet glare.

A large branching oak tree stood close by, its widespread arms affording a pool of welcoming shade. Owen struggled stiffly to his feet and, dragging the Wolfeslayer's body behind him, staggered under the umbrella of purple leaves. He propped his unconscious friend against the midnight dark bole of the huge trunk and shook him gently. Wolfe's head rolled forward on his barrel chest but he showed no signs of recovering consciousness.

"Come on, Wolfe," pleaded Owen, slapping the drained face. "Wake up."

"Leave him," drawled a sardonic voice close by. "He will recover in his own good time."

Owen looked about in surprise. There was no-one in sight.

"Don't worry," yawned the voice. "He is not injured. Leave him be. The rest will do him good."

"Who are you?" demanded Owen curtly. The pounding in his head made him short-tempered. "*Where* are you?"

"I am here, Golden-Arm. Above you."

Owen squinted up into the overhang of leaves.

A man in a wicker cage hung, suspended by one foot, from the topmost branch. His skin had been burnt to almost the same colour as his scarlet clothing. A green halo flared from his flaming hair. It was the Hanged Man from the Tara Cards.

"Greetings, Golden-Arm," he chuckled, clearly amused by Owen's unbelieving stare. "Who are you, if I may ask? And what do you seek in Tara?"

Owen answered without thinking.

"I am Owen Lightbringer and I seek the Magic Iron Ring."

"Do you indeed? Why?"

"Why not?" said the Lightbringer, recovering from his initial surprise. "Since you are so full of questions, let me ask you one. What makes you so interested in my business?"

"You flatter yourself, Golden-Arm," said the Hanged Man, huffily. "Your business is a matter of supreme indifference to me. I merely thought I might be of some assistance. But if you have no need of help . . ." He folded his arms across his scarlet chest and closed his eyes.

"Forgive me," Owen apologised. "I didn't mean to be rude. Please don't go to sleep on me. Agador knows I should be very grateful of any help you can give me."

"I should think so too," grunted the Hanged Man, opening his eyes again. "Now. You were saying. Your reasons for wanting the Iron Ring . . ."

"I need it to awaken my betrothed, the Princess Aneira. Long ago she was placed in a serum-induced trance by the Serpent People of the Tiered City. Only the Magic Ring will revive her."

"Ahhh, love . . ." sighed the human chrysallis. "A noble sentiment . . . but hardly one which justifies so desperate a venture as a trip to the Netherworld. There is more to this quest than mere love, I think."

"Yes," admitted Owen, "there is more, but it is difficult to know where to begin."

"Try the beginning," suggested the Hanged Man.

"Very well," said Owen, taking a deep breath. "I am the Son of the Sun. My father was Zoltan, last of the Sun-Kings. Aneira and I are the only surviving members of the line. Unless we produce an heir the dynasty dies with us . . ."

The Lightbringer touched the heavy sword that hung at his waist, a great two-edged weapon whose hilt carried runic inscriptions, the meaning of which had been lost in the veils of Time.

"This is the Sword of Infinity," he continued. "Tradition-

ally wielded by the Sun-King. Such is its power, it may never be permitted to fall into the wrong hands.

"When a Sun-King dies, his earthly body is transported to the Pyramid of Anakrion. Normally the Sword is passed down from Father to Son on the deathbed. But should the possessor die heirless, his spirit is held in thrall until a successor comes to claim the Sword. The spirit itself does not age, but the body that encases it decays with each passing day, suffering all the rigours of advancing age with no hope of the oblivion of death.

"Without a son, that is my future. Living death after earthly life." He shuddered. "I saw my Father after only twenty years of such bondage. I do not count myself a coward, but it is a fate to which I cannot look forward with much equanimity."

The Hanged Man nodded sagely. "Hmmmmm," he said. "Very interesting."

"I'm glad you find it so," said the Lightbringer dryly.

"I say interesting, Golden-Arm, because obviously you haven't thought about this matter very deeply."

"What do you mean? I think about practically nothing else."

"You say Aneira is the last surviving female of the line? So what of your Son? Whom will he marry? You will pass the Sword of Infinity on to him and save yourself from this fate worse than death. But in doing so, you will lay that fate on him."

Owen felt as though someone had doused him in icy water.

"Great Agador," he groaned. "I hadn't thought of that."

"Evidently," mused the Hanged Man. "A disturbing riddle, is it not?"

"So the old woman was right," gasped Owen. "She said you would pose me a riddle. A riddle that would make my journey to Tara a hollow one. She foresaw it all . . . a riddle to which there would be no solution."

"Well, of course there is a solution," snorted the Hanged Man. "There is a solution to every riddle. But it is a dangerous solution," he added craftily. "And I may give you only half the answer."

"Why?" demanded Owen.

"Because otherwise it would be too easy," tittered the Hanged Man. A sudden puff of wind stirred the leaves of the giant tree. It caught the wicker cage and spun it round like a top.

"The one you seek is in Tara," said the voice from the centre of the whirligig.

"Who is she?" Owen wanted to know.

"The mate . . . wife . . . spouse . . . whatever you wish to call her," puffed the Hanged Man, as the cage gradually slowed down and stopped, "for your non-existent son. She is Astra, Danu's ward."

"You realise it must be someone descended directly from the Sun?"

"And so she is. Better. She is descended from a thousand suns. She is a child of the Universe. A falling star whose downward path brought her to Tara and the clutches of the Temptress. With her genes you could open up your dynasty to encompass Infinity and beyond. But I warn you, Danu has other plans for her. And Danu is not an entity to be trifled with."

"And where do I find this Star-Child?"

"In the same place in which you will find the Magic Iron Ring. In the Palace of Dreams . . . wherein lies every man's destiny . . . and his heart's desire. In your case it is the Ring of Tara. In your son's case, it will be the Fallen Star . . ."

"How poetical." Wolfe's voice interrupted.

"Isn't it though?" sighed the upsidedown figure. "You are recovered I see."

"Have been for some time," said Wolfe gruffly. "I've been listening in on this mad conversation and taking in this mad country. And I've been thinking, you both seem to have overlooked something . . ."

"Indeed? What?"

"The Time factor. Suppose . . . just suppose, we find this Magic Ring? Suppose we ever get it out of here and back to Stonehenge? Suppose Aneira revives . . . Owen marries her . . . they have a child . . . a Son . . .? Suppose when he comes of age we inform him that his ladylove is waiting for him here in the Palace of Dreams? By that time his ladylove will be rather long in the tooth will she not? That is, always supposing she hasn't already married somebody else."

"That's true," said Owen hopelessly. "What do you say to that, Hanged Man?"

"I say your friend is very astute. I say that he has hit upon the other part of the riddle. The half that you must solve for yourself." And he closed his eyes to indicate that, as far as he was concerned, the conversation was at an end.

"Now what?" asked Wolfe.

"To the Palace of Dreams, I suppose," said Owen, sounding far from enthusiastic.

"Which way?"

"I don't know. The Hanged Man didn't say."

"You didn't ask," retorted the human bat, opening one eye. "Through the valley of the Shadow and over the mountains of the Moon . . . by way of the Badenoch pass."

"Is it far?"

"Far enough. A day and a night's ride. The Graal will take you." And he closed his eyes again.

"The Graal?"

Owen looked questioningly at Wolfe, who shrugged his shoulders.

"Here she comes now," observed the Hanged Man, without bothering to open his eyes again.

And out of the trees at the edge of the clearing, an animal came padding.

About the height and roughly twice the length of a small pony, she was covered in shaggy pink fur. Her feline head with tufted ears and oval, grey eyes, was set on a long, stalk-like neck. Her splayed feet, of which there were six, were divided roughly into three sections — two toes in front and one at the back. Each toe was tipped with a silver claw. Just below her neck hung a kangaroo pouch bulging with food and linen. Over her long, broad back was draped a woven blanket of bright blue cloth shot with silver threads.

"Now I've seen everything," muttered Wolfe, nervously. "I hope it doesn't bite."

The Graal halted as she drew abreast of the tree, and lowering her head, nuzzled Wolfe's ear playfully.

"Get off," he shouted, swatting at her ineffectually.

The Graal apparently took these gestures as encouragement for she stared fondly into Wolfe's anguished face and began to drone like a bee. Finally she produced a dark blue tongue of enormous length and proceeded to wash his face with it.

"I think she likes you, Wolfe," laughed Owen, as his unfortunate friend covered his damp face with his hands. "You always did have a way with animals."

"Do not be afraid," chuckled the Hanged Man. "She is quite gentle. You will find food and bedding for your journey in the Graal's neck pouch." He closed his eyes for the final time. "Goodbye," he yawned. "We shall not meet again . . . this time around."

And he began to snore gently.

"Ever had the uncomfortable feeling that you were expected?" asked Wolfe, inspecting the contents of the neck pouch.

"Don't complain," said Owen. "It's better than walking."

And he swung himself up onto the Graal's broad back. When Wolfe had struggled up behind, the animal set off along the valley floor at a brisk, loping trot.

They were about to plunge into the curtain of trees when the Hanged Man hurled one parting verbal shot.

"Oh, by the way," he called, sleepily. "Look out for the Wolfe of Badenoch." And promptly dozed off again.

FIVE

The Wolfe of Badenoch

They emerged from the forest at dusk. The ochre sky had turned dull brown and was shot here and there with lavender highlights.

As they forded a river, whose waters ran red as a dying warrior's blood, the tired sun gave up its attempt to stay awake. It plummeted in a sudden rush behind the jagged mountains, engulfing the strange otherworld of Tara in a darkness that brought with it the dense cold of a desert nightfall.

The dirty green moon, when it rose, brought scant comfort. Its pale, watery rays shed little light in the nightmare gloom.

They camped in a cleft in the rocks at the foot of the Mountains of the Moon. Entering the narrow tunnel, they disturbed a transparent frog with frilled wings. It flapped away under the Graal's clawed feet.

Wolfe, being the expert in living rough, set about building a fire while Owen tethered their steed to a nearby shrub. She stood submissively while Owen relieved her of the refreshments and bedrolls that dragged her neck-pouch down like a greedy pelican's maw, then turned her attention to the rough scrubgrass that carpeted their temporary home. She tore the unsavoury stuff up in great wadges, rumbling it round her mouth with apparent relish.

Owen was frozen to the marrow. Wistfully, he thought of his furlined cloak which lay, where Wolfe had dropped it, outside the entrance to the Long Barrow of Kilken. Unrolling one of the heavy, hide blankets, he threw it gratefully round his shoulders and took a long drink from the wooden water bottle that had been concealed inside. The liquid was strong and sweet. It coursed through his veins in a warm surge, leaving him instantly revived.

"C-c-c-curse this c-c-cold," complained Wolfe, trying, without success, to control his chattering teeth. "My fingers are all thumbs."

He scraped awkwardly at his tinderflint, coaxing a spark from it with frozen fingers. It fell on the damp wood which began to smoulder fitfully.

"Here," said Owen. "Try some of this. It'll make you feel better."

Wolfe downed an enormous draught of the fiery brew.

"By Agador, that's good stuff," he snorted. "I wouldn't mind the recipe. Here. Let's see if it has the same effect on the fire as it's had on me," and he sloshed a thimbleful of the liquid onto the sputtering logs.

A whoosh of flame shot skywards, setting the fire sparking and crackling. The resultant light threw grotesquely enlarged shadows on the purple walls that hemmed them in.

"That's better," said Wolfe, crouching down and holding his hands out to the blaze. "Now. What's to eat?"

"Bread, dried meat and some sort of fruit," said Owen, unwrapping the packages one by one. "Not very inspiring but sufficient to keep us going."

"What I wouldn't give for a nice drop of jackrat stew." Wolfe licked his lips. The moisture froze immediately, forming a crystal crust over his mouth. "If it wasn't so freezing, I'd go and see if I couldn't catch some fresh meat."

A bloodcurdling howl split the night silence. Eerie. Inhuman. It began as a low moan and rose to a shriek that sent shivers across the moon.

The Graal raised her head from her evening meal, snorting through nostrils flared with fear.

"Something stalks tonight," said Owen grimly. "Despite the weather."

"Wolfe call," said the Wolfeslayer, a hunter's gleam appearing in his eye. "I'd know that sound anywhere. And hungry, too, if I'm not very much mistaken."

"Look out for the Wolfe of Badenoch," muttered Owen.

"Eh?"

"Nothing. I was just thinking aloud."

Another baying howl split the dark, closer this time and punctuated by a shrill scream of pain.

The Graal gave a whinny of pure terror and began to strain against her binding rope. Owen left the warmth of the fire to stroke the frightened animal's muzzle.

"There, there, you are safe with us," he crooned, reassuringly.

But the fearful sound came again, breaking in on his soothing words and echoing round the walls of their narrow shelter with unmistakeable menace.

The Graal began to buck and plunge in a crazed frenzy. Ignoring Owen's efforts to calm her, she tore the shrub up by its roots and, trailing it behind her, lumbered off into the night.

Without a word, the Sun-Prince flung aside his blanket and rushed after her.

"Owen . . . stop . . ." protested Wolfe, but the Lightbringer had already disappeared into the blackness beyond the cranny's entrance.

"Silly young perisher," he muttered. "He'll never find her out there . . . just as well he's got the Sword with him . . . but what's the point in my talking . . . one word from me and he does as he likes . . . sometimes I wonder why I bother . . . wild goose chase . . . if he'd any sense he'd stay here and have his supper . . . like me . . ."

His voice trailed away as the hairs on the back of his neck began to rise, one by one, away from skin that was suddenly clammy with sweat.

It was an unmistakeable feeling. Wolfe had experienced it many times in his years as a skin-trapper.

He was being watched.

With infinite caution, so as not to disturb whatever it was that was eyeing him, he edged away from the rock wall and looked over his shoulder.

Perched on a narrow ledge, directly above him, was an enormous, black hellhound. Dripping fangs bared in a fierce

grimace, it crouched, ready to spring. Its sleek, muscular body glowed in the surrounding darkness as though each bristling hair had been tipped with phosphorescent paint. The curved claws, razor sharp as an eagle's, were stained dark by the blood of a recent victim.

And the eyes . . .

The eyes were pure fire. Deep red and seething with malice.

A picture formed in Wolfe's paralysed brain. A great black Sword on a background of blood and over it the words of the old crone taunted him.

"Death . . . It stalks you in many forms . . . I see a hound with eyes of coal . . ."

He reached for the killing-knife he kept concealed in his boot and backed up towards the fire.

"Well, Wolfeslayer," he muttered. "It's a long time since you lived up to your name . . . Now's your chance to see if the old skills are still there . . . Come on, you brute!" he yelled. "I'm ready when you are . . ."

And with a low growl, the monster sprang.

Wolfe fell into a crouch, to lessen the impact. As the black beast catapulted into him, he managed to slip his left arm around the creature's hairy neck. Then they were rolling over and over on the prickly scrubgrass, Wolfe fighting frantically to keep the snapping jaws away from his throat.

Using its superior weight, the great animal managed to regain its feet. It shrugged Wolfe off as it might shrug off a few drops of rain, and turning with a savage snarl, buried its teeth in its adversary's shoulder. Wolfe yelled in pain as he felt the bones crunch under the beast's grip.

With all the strength he could muster, he aimed his knife at the hound's soft underbelly.

But the wolfe was worrying him like a jackrat. The constant jiggling knocked his aim off so that instead of plunging into vulnerable flesh, the knife merely ricocheted off a rib.

With a startled yelp, the wolfe opened its jaws and writhed away, wrenching the knife from the Wolfeslayer's hand. The weapon clattered harmlessly to the ground.

Wolfe struggled to sit up. His left arm hung uselessly beneath the shattered shoulder.

Thick, black blood spurted from the shallow wound in the hound's side. It sniffed the cut unbelievingly, then with a shriek of anger, raked its claws down the side of the Wolfe-slayer's face. A set of bloody furrows opened in the flesh running from forehead to chin and missing the left eye by a hairsbreadth. The fury of the blow knocked him in a back somersault through the pile of smouldering embers. Dazed and bleeding, he tried to get to his knees. The copious flow of blood from the cuts on his face ran into his eyes, almost blinding him. Through the crimson waterfall his knife winked tantalisingly at him across the fire, too far away now to be of any use.

The great, black beast eyed the injured man warily across the glowing ashes and, keeping a fair distance from the occasional licking flame, began to stalk slowly round towards him. Wolfe, in turn, shuffled backwards, attempting to keep the fire between the advancing animal and himself.

They circled like this for some little time. The slashes in Wolfe's face had begun to throb and the pain in his shoulder was becoming unbearable. He gritted his teeth. Flashes of light began to dance in front of his eyes. He knew if he didn't do something soon, he'd pass out.

He began to talk to himself.

"Not much of a showing so far," he admonished. "Crawling around like a snake in the grass. Stand up. I'm ashamed of you. Get up off your knees and fight like a man."

But it was no good. He couldn't see properly. He didn't know what he was doing. He could feel himself falling . . .

Then he was awake again, or half-awake, vaguely aware

that the hound had him pinned to the ground with its fore-paws. He could feel the stench of its fetid breath in his face.

In a last desperate attempt to save himself, he scrabbled among the ashes for a burning firebrand meaning to thrust it into the wolfe's coal-red eyes. But in the event he was unequal to the task and only succeeded in scorching his fingers.

The slavering jaws were an inch from his exposed throat when a cry from the mouth of the tiny gulley pulled the beast up short. It bounced off the walls in an amplified challenge.

"AGADOR VANZORIBUS."

The battle cry of the Sun-Kings.

Through pain-misted eyes, the Wolfeslayer glimpsed the fearsome figure of Owen Lightbringer bearing down on the great, black beast.

He held the Sword of Infinity in his golden hand and Man and Weapon were wreathed in the Sacred Fire of the Sun. Both were charged with an elemental force that was as invincible as it was awe-inspiring.

Wolfe felt the weight on his chest lessen as, with a spine-chilling howl, the Wolfe of Badenoch hurled itself at the approaching apparition.

The Sun-Prince lifted his golden arm to strike the killing blow.

And Wolfe, overcome at last by the pain, slithered quietly into unconsciousness.

SIX

The Flame of Life

The man with the wild, white hair looked up from the anvil as the dwarf entered and made the sign of obeisance. He set aside the iron wand with which he had been fashioning a copper amulet and wiped the back of his hand across his high domed forehead. The heat in the small cave was intense. Behind him the never-cooling fire of the forge flickered with a deep blue flame.

The dwarf, dressed for the outside in garments fashioned from animal hair, had the bright pink complexion of a cooked shrimp. Under his sweating armpit he carried a ragged parcel wrapped in hessian.

"Well, Foodhunter?" asked the big man. "Did the chase go well?"

"Reasonably well, Giobnhu," replied the dwarf. "Two porcupiles, a llamandra and one of Danu's Graals. But I have something else to report. We have taken two prisoners . . . from the Otherside."

"Indeed? Much trouble?"

"None. We found them in the east cleft at the foot of the Badenoch Pass. The older one is badly wounded. The other, though he could have taken all six of us easily, seemed demoralised by his friend's condition. He offered no resis-

tance. He is a curious specimen. A golden arm and a mark like a rising sun on his forehead. Strange eyes . . . like a Tigra . . . and that's not all . . ."

"Well, well?" said Giobnhu impatiently. "Spit it out."

"He has killed the wolfe."

"What? I don't believe it."

"I feared you might not, so I brought this along as proof."

The dwarf leant forward and, without bending his stubby legs, placed the parcel on the ground. The crude wrappings fell away like petals dropping from a wilted flower. In their centre lay the severed head of the black Wolfe of Badenoch. The red eyes, dulled now in death, still held the imprint of disbelief the beast had felt as the fatal blow struck. The black tongue lolled from the open mouth as though panting in the suffocating heat of the forge.

"A clean slice," said Foodhunter. "As you can see."

"Impossible," said the Magician-Smith, turning the grisly relic over with his toe, the better to examine the wound. "The weapon has not been forged that could strike such a blow . . . unless . . . did either of them carry a sword?"

"The young one. A great iron sword with strange markings on the handle."

"What kind of markings?"

"Runes. Indecipherable. I have not seen their like before . . . except . . ."

"Except where?"

"On the inside of the Ring, Giobnhu. The inscription. And only you know the meaning of that."

Giobnhu's eyes glittered in the flamelight.

"Of course," he muttered. "The Golden Arm . . . Can it be? After all this time?" He pulled himself together. "Where is this young man?" he demanded.

"In the Hospice . . . with his companion. The Healeress is with them, but I fear there is little hope . . . he lost much blood on the way."

"Take me to them."

"At once, Giobnhu."

Foodhunter scuttled out into the main workshops and, pausing only to retrieve his iron wand, Giobnhu followed, ducking his white head as he passed beneath the smoke-scorched lintel.

The forges of Giobnhu lay in the very heart of the Mountains of the Moon. The central workshop was a hive of activity. Small fires burned at intervals around a great borehole in which white-hot lava danced a bubbling jig.

Dwarf-workers scurried between the fires like demented ants, each one engrossed in some specific activity.

All were dressed alike in loose-fitting purple garments, light in texture as befitted the temperature. Some had padded gauntlets, others transparent, amber eyemasks, but without exception they all wore the thick leather apron of the Iron-Smith, divided into pocketed compartments from which bristled the tools of their trade.

Foodhunter led his master through the bustle to a small alcove at the far end of the chamber. Its walls were lined with potions and bottles of healing-herbs. A bowl of scented fluid, brimful with a brace of marinating poultices, lay on an outcropping of rock, within arms' reach of the tiny yellow-clad figure of the Healeress. Beside her, a tall, handsome youth with corn-coloured hair stood looking on helplessly.

The sick man lay on a floating airbed. His body was almost rigid and the skin had taken on the livid pallor of a corpse. His crushed right shoulder was stained carmine with caked blood and a set of fearsome scars ran down one side of his face.

The young man looked up at their approach. The Sun-Mark on his forehead seemed to leap at them through the gloom.

"You have killed my watchdog, stranger," accused Giobnhu gruffly. "Explain yourself."

"Your watchdog has sorely injured one who meant him no harm," retorted the young man heatedly. "Explain that."

"It is regrettable. The precautions were not meant for you but for Danu's Pawns. Still, you were found snooping around one of the secret entrances to the Mountains of the Moon. Our work is private here. You have no-one but yourselves to blame."

"We were not snooping. We were on our way to the Palace of Dreams with no thought of the Mountains of the Moon, except that we needed to cross them to get to our destination. Who are you that you presume so much? What work can possibly justify such a barbarous means of guarding it?"

"I am Giobnhu," roared the Magician-Smith. "Master here. Who are you, upstart intruder?"

"I am Owen Lightbringer, Son of the Sun. Willing to challenge your mastery when you please."

"If you must quarrel, do it elsewhere," said the Healeress, looking up under her cowl with stern, green eyes. "This man is dying. The least you can do is to let him die in peace."

"Dying?" The young man was incredulous. "He cannot be dying. He is a Twice-Born."

"On the Otherside perhaps," said the Healeress sharply. "But here, in Tara, things are different. Our life-force negates yours. See. His wounds are real enough. Had he been Twice-Born they would have healed instantly. No. In Tara he is mortal. In Tara, he is dying."

"Is there nothing you can do for him?"

The Healeress shook her head.

"He is beyond my help. Only Giobnhu can save him now . . . It is his choice."

"His choice?" shouted the Lightbringer furiously. "It is his duty. But for his cursed hound, Wolfe would not be in this condition." He put his hand threateningly on the great iron sword at his waist. "Do what you can for him Smith . . . I demand it."

A shocked silence fell in the tiny compartment.

Then the dwarf, Foodhunter, spoke.

"You dare address yourself thus to the great Giobnhu?" he hissed. "Master. But say the word and I will slit this Buzzcock's throat."

"No, no," said Giobnhu, placing a hand on Foodhunter's pumpkin head. "I can deal with this myself. Who knows? I may even be able to save this young man's friend . . . for a consideration."

"What do you mean?" demanded the Sun-Prince.

"I mean an exchange. His life . . . for your sword."

"My Sword?"

"It is the Sword of Infinity, is it not?"

"It is."

The Smith licked his lips greedily.

"Then I have need of it."

"You disillusion me, Giobnhu." Scorn stained the young man's golden eyes. "Legend tells that the Magician-Smith of Tara is just and wise. Not one to bargain with life like a common Sorceror. But you shall have the Sword . . . if your desire for it is so great."

He drew the weapon from its jewelled scabbard.

Immediately a strange, dancing fire surrounded man and sword, fizzling about them like Summer lightning.

With a startled squeak, Foodhunter hid himself in the folds of his master's red cloak. The Healeress pulled her cowl low to protect her startled green eyes from the glare. Only Giobnhu continued to stare at the apparition.

Owen flipped the great Sword over. It described a flaming arc in the furnace-hot air before landing, tip downwards in his golden hand, its hilt presented towards the Magician.

Giobnhu reached to grasp the handle in his ham-like fist.

But the Sword had ideas of its own. It uttered a demented screech and began to quiver with suppressed fury. As the Smith wrapped his fingers around it, the hilt turned red hot. He dropped it with a howl of pain and, as the weapon slid, of its own volition, back into the scabbard, the bright, white fire died away.

"My apologies," said Owen. "It appears the Sword wishes no part of such a bargain."

"So I see," said Giobnhu wryly, blowing on his scorched fingers. "But it is I who should apologise. I don't know what came over me. In truth I did not intend to keep it. I have no use for the Sword itself. It is the runes I am after, especially the ones on the blade. I had hoped to learn something from them. Something to improve my craft. Though I must admit," he added wistfully, "it would have been something to have held it in my hand. The Sword of Infinity. The greatest weapon ever forged."

"But the meaning of the runes has been lost in the mists of Time," protested Owen. "Even I do not understand them."

"No, Sun-Prince, for if you could decipher them they would make no sense to you. They are in code. A craftsman's code. A code for which only I hold the key. The secret has been passed down through generations of Alchemists against the day when one of us should come in contact with the Sword again. And now that day has come . . . and with my bungling, I have lost the chance."

"What is this code?" asked Owen curiously.

"It is a secret formula that will temper a sword blade so that the edge will never blunt . . . and turn the basest dross into gold."

"Well then, I will write it out for you," promised the Sun-Prince. "I know the rune patterns by heart. You shall have them if you save the Wolfeslayer."

"You shame me, Lightbringer," said Giobnhu. "I will save your friend. But one thing you should know in advance. If he passes through the Flame of Life, he will become, as you call it, a Twice-Born, here in Tara. If and when you return to the Otherside, the process will be reversed. In your space-time continuum, he will be a mere mortal again."

"Then I shall have to take more care of him there than I have done here," said the Sun-Prince. "Do what you must."

"Bring him," ordered the Magician, and with Foodhunter manouvering the airbed through the press of busy workers, Giobnhu led Owen to the rim of the huge natural cauldron that pulsed in the centre of the main workshop.

"This will look fearsome," he warned. "But your companion will feel no pain."

With a gentle push, he propelled the airbed out over the molten furnace. The hot currents lifted it like a leaf, high into the air. It hovered, rocking gently, halfway between the seething pit and the roof.

Giobnhu took the iron wand from his belt and pointed it towards the fire.

A grumbling sounded in the bowels of the mountain and the ground began to tremble beneath Owen's feet.

One by one the dwarves downed tools and clustered around the edge of the inferno.

Then, with a great whooshing roar, a column of dark blue fire shot upwards from the centre to envelop the airbed and its occupant in a sheet of living flame.

It was an awesome sight. And awe was stamped upon the sea of upturned faces that were reflected in the eerie, blue flame-light.

"Tell me, Son of the Sun," said Giobnhu quietly. "What do you seek in the Palace of Dreams?"

And Owen explained, without once taking his eyes from the tiny figure bobbing in the eye of the holocaust, his search for the Ring and his reasons for wanting it.

Giobnhu listened without interruption until the Lightbringer finished.

"Well, I wish you luck," he said then. "But I tell you now, that Danu will not relinquish the Ring lightly. Think not to touch her heart with your story, for she has no heart. I made the Ring for her in happier times. She promised that she would use it for the common good. Instead she kept it for herself. She is old now. Old and vain, and the Ring is the source of her continuing youth. With its magic powers she surrounds herself with a pattern of false vibrations. They show her to be young and beautiful. As she once was. As she would always be. She has become a corrupt and evil tyrant. She even threatens me. And there is no disposing of her. In our closer days I was foolish enough to allow her to pass through the Flame of Life."

As if at a signal, the Flame died, as suddenly as it had risen, dropping back into the heart of the fire like a spent force.

The Magician-Smith took a small magnet from the folds of his scarlet cloak. He directed its beam towards the airbed which drifted down until it hung before them, quivering like an eager dog awaiting orders.

On its inflated mattress Wolfe lay breathing gently. The disfiguring wounds had disappeared without trace and his skin had taken on the pink glow of restored health. He slept peacefully as a contented child.

SEVEN

The Palace of Dreams

As they came out into the dying sunlight, Foodhunter pulled the tinted visor low over his cave-weakened eyes.

"This is as far as I go," he said, "Giobnhu's servants are no longer welcome in Danu's domain."

The City of Tara lay spread beneath them like an embroidered eiderdown in whose elaborate centre stood the Palace of Dreams. To Owen it looked like a diadem spun from stars, with its tall crystal spires and filigreed parapets glinting like a clutch of jewelled eggs in the setting sun.

It reminded Wolfe of the Fairgrounds of his boyhood, all striped awnings and fluttering flags. While to Foodhunter it appeared no more than a gigantic mound of earth riddled with entrance holes like a collossal porcupile warren.

For no two people saw the Palace alike. Each created it in the image of his own desire. It was what one wished it to be. The Palace of Dreams.

Foodhunter held out a small, horny hand to each of his companions in turn.

"I wish you fortune," he said, "And offer you one piece of advice. Never turn your back on Danu. Now I must be going. Giobnhu will have need of me. He's so obsessed with his

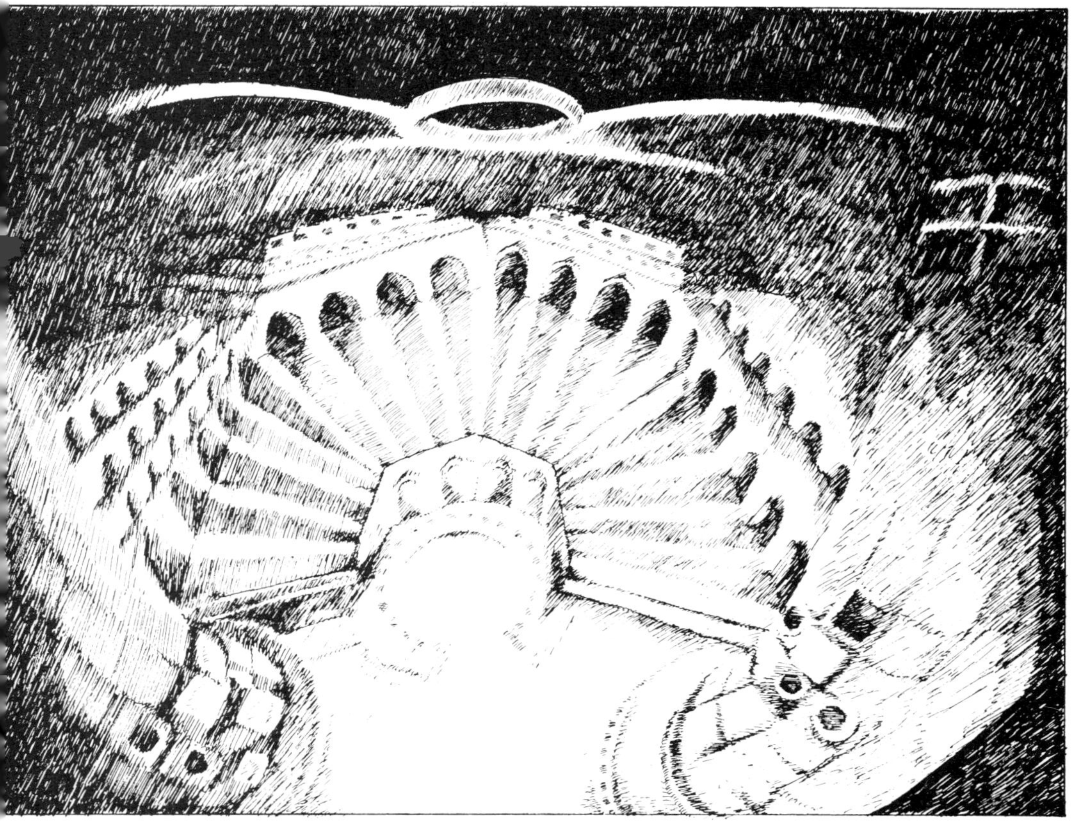

rune-markings, he'll forget to eat unless I'm there to remind him."

And, turning on his heel he disappeared back into the hole in the mountain.

Owen and Wolfe reached the carved gateway to Tara City as twilight was drawing a veil across the streets. Darkness descended as it had done at the foot of the Badenoch Pass, with alarming suddenness. And it brought with it the same biting cold.

The two friends were grateful for the functional if inelegant coverings that the dwarves had hastily stitched together from several of their own cloaks. It had taken three to accommodate the stocky bulk of the Wolfeslayer, four for the taller Lightbringer. They pulled the makeshift garments around them and hurried into the thronged thoroughfare.

None of the inhabitants, each one intent on gaining the warmth of his own hearthstone, appeared to notice the two strangers in their midst. They were a dour lot. Here and there the occasional sound of revelry filtered through a tavern door, but otherwise the citizens of Tara went on their respective ways in grim silence.

Owen and Wolfe strode through the maze of cobbled walkways towards the slight incline that led up to Danu's Palace. Even taking into account the swift drop in temperature, the streets had emptied with amazing rapidity.

As they turned a sharp corner into a particularly narrow alley, the reason for the sudden exodus became abundantly clear.

They had accidentally strayed into a cul-de-sac. At the far end, a group of young men, dissipation stamped on their pimply features, lounged around a torch-bearing pole. This rickety contraption shed a watery light on the muddy craters and miscellaneous detritus that made up the surface of the road.

As Owen and Wolfe rounded the corner, the desultory hum of conversation died away and all eyes turned in their direction.

The tallest of the gang, a youth of about Owen's age, detached himself from the group and strutted arrogantly into the centre of the street. His black, greasy hair was caught in a horsetail over one ear, half-concealing the death-beetle scar that deformed his right cheek. His heavy, leather gloves were liberally studded with sharp, metal spikes. A sliver of bone pierced the septum of his broken nose.

"Well, well, well," he sneered. "Lost our way have we, gents? What a pity. Maybe we can be of 'elp?" He smiled a mirthless smile. The cicatrice scar puckered alarmingly.

"Then again, maybe we can't," he sniggered, placing two fingers in his mouth and whistling through broken teeth.

Owen glanced briefly over his shoulder. As he'd anticipated, several more unsavoury characters were sliding out of the shadows behind them, effectively cutting off their retreat.

"We can give you some directions though, can't we boys?"

A shout of raucous laughter greeted this remark, peppered with suggestions as to where the directions might lead.

"But times are hard," continued the gang-boss. "I'm afraid we'll need paying for our information. Got any money, have we gents?"

Languidly, he unwrapped a length of heavy chain from around his waist and began to swing it threateningly from side to side. Then, with the speed of a striking serpent, his hand shot forward, cracking the metal rope like a whip under Owen's nose. It missed his upper lip by a hairsbreadth. A smattering of applause followed this display of ferocity.

"Bloodthirsty bunch," muttered Wolfe under his breath. "What say we teach them a lesson?"

"No," said Owen firmly. "You've only just recovered from one fight. You're hardly ready to embark on another."

"Let me be the judge of that," growled Wolfe, slipping the killing-knife from his boot.

"We want no trouble," said Owen, addressing the swaggering, tattooed figure before him. "But if you insist on it, I should warn you, my companion here is a Twice-Born, and I am not entirely without experience in the art of combat."

"Not entirely without experience, aren't we?" mimicked the gang-leader. "Can't say as 'ow I'm impressed. As for your friend being a Twice-Born, wot's that when it's at 'ome? Anyway, 'oo mentioned fightin'? Not me. Most unsociable I call it. Don't you, Vultures?"

A muttered chorus of affirmation rumbled round the sightless windows of the blind alley.

"I reckon these gents want a lesson in manners. Shall we give 'em one?"

And without waiting for a reply, he stalked towards the Lightbringer, hefting the length of chain lovingly in one gloved hand.

Following his lead, the crowd of cutpurses began to close in on all sides.

Wolfe reached in his belt for the studded mace he kept there. But he could not anticipate the blow that sent him reeling into the nearest darkened doorway. It came, not from the expected quarter, but from his companion's fist. The Sun-Prince's savage uppercut caught him directly in the stomach. He collapsed into the peeling paintwork of the crumbling stairwell.

"Stay there," shouted the Lightbringer. And Wolfe was, for once, too winded to disobey.

Backing up so that his body shielded Wolfe from the advancing felons, Owen flung aside his ill-fitting cloak and tore the Sword of Infinity from its scabbard.

The fire of the Sun-Kings sent the shadows scurrying to safety and stopped the Vultures in their tracks.

The Lightbringer extended his golden arm until the tip of the flaming Sword rested lightly on the leading youth's unmarked cheek. He nodded at the scarred side.

"How would you like another one to match?" he asked, silkily.

Silence descended on the alley, broken only by the scraping of studded boots and the stentorian breathing of Wolfe from the doorway.

Finally, the leading Vulture spoke.

"Okay, lads," he said nervously. "Leave this one out."

And, like sinners fleeing the plague, the gang slithered out of the alley-way, some up drainpipes, some through broken windows, some edging their way along the slimy walls until they were in a position to sidle past the Lightbringer and out into the night.

Soon, the mean street was empty, except for the greasy-haired youth with the broken teeth. Slowly, with infinite caution, he backed away from the flaming sword. Then, in deference to the swashbuckling image he undoubtedly had of himself, he directed a cocky salute at the glowing apparition. With a cheeky "Be seein' you gents," he shinned up the torch-pole, leapt onto the nearest roof and disappeared among the chimney pots.

Owen slid the Sword of Infinity back into its sheath and leant to give his friend a hand up.

"Shortest fight I ever had," complained the Wolfeslayer. "You spoilsport. Don't ever do that to me again."

The road halted abruptly some twenty metres in front of the vaulted doorway that guarded the interior of the Palace of Dreams.

A great trench had been dug around the building and filled with stagnant water. The stench that rose from it indicated that it was little better than an open sewer.

"Now what?" demanded Wolfe. "I don't fancy swimming through that."

But before Owen could reply, the door swung out and downwards in a creaking of unoiled chains, to form a bridge over the noisome canal.

A tall, pale figure hurried across to greet them. He stood out, in the light from the slit-windows, like a child's idea of a phantom. His waxy features were surmounted by lank, dun-coloured hair and his clothes, which sat on him like rags on a witch's dolly, were the same dingy off-white as his skin. A white cap sat uneasily on his egg-shaped head and in one hand he held an ivory stick of office.

When he spoke, his lips didn't move. No hint of an expression wrinkled his blank, bloodless face.

"The Queen is expecting you," he declaimed. "Be so good as to follow me."

EIGHT

Danu

The corridor to the Receiving Room was dim and smelt of damp earth.

The Pawn whirred along in front of them on oiled wheels, his short, white cape flapping behind him. As it rose and fell, it exposed the cavity in his back which housed his inner workings.

The passageway ended in a pair of double-doors set flush in the dark green wall. They swung inwards at a touch from the Pawn's ivory wand and, pausing only to ensure that Owen and Wolfe were still following him, he scuttled through.

The Receiving Room was vast and, after the gloom of the corridor, blindingly lit.

At first Owen thought the great chamber was open to the sky, but, as his eyes adjusted themselves to the glare, he realised that it was a rather clever optical illusion. The roof had been laid out to represent the Universe in reverse, each planet and star formed by a spotlight in the dark blue ceiling.

The floor, on the other hand, had been constructed in a series of black and white squares, exactly like a giant chess-board.

Danu's courtiers stood, singly or in stiff groups, at intervals around the smooth, anthracite walls. They were all, without

exception, white android pawns.

At the far end of the room, on a raised dais, set in an alcove and backed by a great grey machine, the Temptress of Tara awaited them. Both she and the amethyst throne on which she sat, gave off a faint film of ectoplasm.

To her left, on a sloping console, stood an exact replica of the Receiving Room in miniature. It bristled with tiny copies of the Pawns that peopled the actual floor.

To her right, on a padded footstool, sat her Ward, the Star-Child.

The Messenger-Pawn halted, a little more than his own length away from the dais, and fell forward on his broad, white face.

"The visitors you were expecting have arrived, High One," he intoned, the sound emerging from the back of his head.

And, as a sign of respect, Owen and the Wolfeslayer knelt

before the Ruler of the City State of Tara.

Danu was a strikingly beautiful woman of statuesque proportions. Her strong-featured face with its creamy skin and huge violet eyes, was marred only by the petulant droop at the corners of the full mouth. Her shimmery, bronze gown, which mirrored the gleaming thatch of auburn hair, was cut to cling to her generous curves, as closely as decency would allow. She wore no jewellery, except for a plain, iron ring on the third finger of her left hand. The Magic Ring of Tara.

Yet despite, or perhaps because of, her obvious charms, Danu looked coarse and vulgar compared to the small figure who sat so demurely in her shadow.

The Star-Child glowed. Not with the artificial energy that surrounded the Temptress, but with an inner light that shone through her translucent, silver skin. Her eyes, clear and guileless as mountain rock-pools, observed the kneeling strangers with the curious innocence of a fawn that has, as yet, not learnt the meaning of danger.

She wore a pale pink, one-shouldered shift, caught at the waist with a sparkling rope. A wreath of wild roses, in the same delicate colour, held back her veil of silvery hair. She was like a tiny, exquisitely-wrought snowflake.

The rich, plummy tones of the Temptress swooped around the Receiving Room, picked up and amplified by a series of sound boxes set discreetly in the walls.

"So, Prince of the Sun," she said. "We meet again."

Owen did not reply at once. He waited for the command that would allow him to rise from his uncomfortable, kneeling position. But the command never came.

He glanced up and was shocked by the Temptress's brazen stare. But he was not entirely unaffected by it, even though one half of him knew that he was being manipulated.

"The Queen must be mistaken," he stammered. His voice, after the Queen's, sounded feeble in the extreme. "I do not believe I have ever been so privileged . . ."

"The Queen is never mistaken . . ." interrupted Danu, imperiously. "We *have* met before . . . that is how I know you have come for the Ring. But that is of no consequence now. We have much more important things to discuss."

She patted the arm of the amethyst throne invitingly.

"Here," she said with a come-hither smile. "Sit by me."

Owen rose from his knees but made no attempt to ascend the dais.

"I would not so presume, Madam . . ." he protested.

The Temptress fixed him with a sensual stare.

"You might presume much with me, Sun-Prince," she said coyly. "It is a very long time since I encountered so pleasing a young man."

She ran her pink tongue over her full, red lips.

"Brazen hussy!" muttered Wolfe under his breath.

"Can I not persuade you to forget this foolish quest?" wheedled Danu. "Stay here with me, Bringer of Light. I can promise you more — much more — than you will ever get from your sleeping beauty. Riches. Comfort. Luxuries and delights that you have never dreamed of. I offer you all these — and myself— if you will forget Aneira and stay in the Palace of Dreams."

"I regret, Madam," said Owen stiffly, "that my affections are not for sale."

If he had struck the Queen across the face, her reaction could not have been more extreme. Her face whitened and her full lips curled in an unsightly sneer.

"Little man," she said sharply. "You have rejected a proposal that many would die for. Begone! You are wasting my time and yours. Take your miserable face out of my sight."

"But . . . the Ring, Danu . . ." ventured Owen.

"You dare ask me for the Ring now?" said Danu icily. "You shall never have it. I do not choose that your betrothed should awaken."

"But what possible difference can it make? I've already told you I will not stay with you."

"Do not flatter yourself, Lightbringer," smirked the Temptress. "My interest in you was but a secondary consideration. Much more important things are at stake than a passing infatuation."

She leant forward and, for the first time, Owen saw the greed and ambition mirrored in her violet eyes.

"Say, for the sake of argument," she said, "that I *were* to give you the Ring . . . with it you return to the Otherside and wake Aneira from her age-old sleep. You marry . . . she bears a child. If that child is a daughter — well, that is another story — but if that child is a son . . . an Heir to the Sun Dynasty . . . then in time, he too will want to take a bride . . . and I know where he will look. There will be no suitable bride for him in his own space-time continuum. So . . . he will come here — to Tara — to claim the hand of the Star-Child for his own."

The silvery tones of the Star-Maiden interrupted the Temptress's monologue.

"I don't think I would mind that at all, Danu," she smiled. "If this one's son turns out to be half as handsome as he, I should be more than content to marry him. He is much prettier than Cernunnos . . ."

"Be silent, child!" ordered Danu, icily. "You don't know what you're talking about."

"Oh yes I do," chimed in the Star-Child. "I'm talking about my future."

"Enough!" commanded the Temptress. "Allow me to know what is best for you. And kindly do not interrupt again."

With a small, resigned sigh, the Star-Child subsided into silence.

"Your son will want a wife," continued Danu, "and he will

look for her here. But I have other plans for my Ward. She is promised to Cernunnos, the Horned-One.

"Their progeny will combine all the extreme opposites. The light and the dark. The height and the depths. The strong and the gentle. The good and the evil. An irresistible combination."

The amplified voice had become louder and louder during the course of this diatribe. The violet eyes had taken on a hint of insanity. Now Danu raised her voice to a triumphant shout.

"Their child will be invincible," she prophesied. "He will burst forth from the confines of Tara, to take control, first of the Otherside, then of the Universe. And I shall be there to guide him."

"But Danu," interrupted Owen craftily, "all this makes no sense. How *can* my Son hope to make the Star-Child his bride? He is as yet unborn. She will be married long before he comes to Manhood. By the time he goes seeking a bride, it will be too late."

"For a Son of the Sun you are ill-informed," snorted Danu. "Surely you know that Time is one continuous circle? Provided one knows the co-ordinates, one may pierce it at any given moment."

She raised her hand to her mouth in consternation, conscious, too late, of what she had said.

"Thank you, Danu," said Owen quietly. "You have solved the other half of the riddle for me."

"You gloat too soon, upstart!" screeched Danu. "I shall never allow you to leave Tara. I am the Mistress of Time, for I choose what your future will be. In that future, your Son will never be born, your betrothed will never awaken, and I shall be free to pursue my Master-Plan unhindered."

Her left hand, darted towards the console and pressed a red switch. The huge machine behind her began to throb and hum. The tiny Pawns started to move in unison towards the miniature amethyst throne. As they did so, their full-sized counterparts clicked into life and converged on the two kneeling figures.

Hastily, Owen and Wolfe scrambled to their feet.

The Pawns clanked forward. With a sly smile, Danu pressed a purple switch and their right arms fell away with a clatter.

Each of the Pawns now had a weapon where their arms had been. Here a double-headed axe, there a needle-sharp rapier. Pronged forks sprouted from some shoulders, grappling irons from others.

Behind the platoon of Killers came six others. The Restrainers. Only their hands had been discarded. The edges of a heavily-weighted mesh net protruded from the stumps of their wrists.

Danu glared down at the two trapped figures. Her square, white teeth glinted in the fake starlight.

"You are no longer Master of your own Fate, Owen Lightbringer," she pronounced. "You . . . and the Sun Dynasty . . . end here . . ."

NINE

The Fire Chariot

The sword-armed Pawn lunged for Owen's throat. Wolfe leapt in front of the Sun-Prince and parried the blow with his upstretched arm. It almost cut the limb in two. But before the blood could gush from the wound, it had already begun to heal, bone knitting perfectly to bone, flesh melding into flesh.

There was a gasp of surprise from the Star-Maiden and a grunt of agony from Wolfe. Being a Twice-Born might guarantee immortality, but it did not preclude pain, even though any wounds inflicted healed with miraculous speed.

The interlude gave Owen the time he needed to draw the Sword of Infinity. As it left the scabbard, the fire of the Sun-Kings flowed around Man and Weapon, joining them together in one invincible fighting machine. The cold, white flame lit up the over-bright room with an ever brighter glow.

Wolfe whipped the killing-knife from his boot and the small, studded mace from his belt and took up his customary fighting position, two paces behind the Lightbringer, slightly to his left.

And then the Machine-Men were upon them.

Owen took the first one's head off with a swish of the giant sword. Springs and cog-wheels catapulted from the neck like firecrackers.

But the Pawn did not fall. Instead its headless trunk began to whirl about in an aimless waltz. It careered around, crashing into the other Pawns. And as its body ricocheted about, its severed head sent out a senselessly-repeated message.

"Kill them, kill them, kill them, kill them, kill them!"

Danu jabbed a switch on the console and the rogue Pawn puttered to a halt. She flicked another and the rest of her mechanised guards pressed in with renewed intensity.

"Go for their backs, Wolfe!" shouted Owen. "If we can disrupt the circuits . . ."

Wolfe darted behind a mace-wielder and plunged his killing knife up to the wrist in the back cavity.

There was a series of short, sharp explosions and the Pawn fell apart. The synthetic stuff that made up its pseudo-skin began to liquify and run down the metal limbs like candle drippings.

Furiously, Danu twiddled knobs and pulled switches.

But the Machine-Men, though very much stronger, lacked the manoeuvrability of their human counterparts. Again and again Owen and Wolfe managed to evade their blows, slip under their guard and disrupt their clockwork insides. Soon a smell of burnt-out circuits and a heap of spare parts were all that remained of the fighting men.

Owen was polishing off the last of the rapier-pawns, taking his time, enjoying the cut and thrust of the contest, when a cry from the Wolfeslayer pulled him up short.

He turned to look over his shoulder, parrying, more by instinct than by sight, a thrust from his opponent's rapier arm.

Foolishly he had forgotten the Restrainers.

Now Wolfe was trapped, enmeshed in the gigantic net they had thrown out. He thrashed about helplessly like a dragonfly in a tarantula's web, while the Pawns circled him in formation, mechanical dancers around a human Maypole.

Owen smashed the two-edged Sword down through the centre of his unsuspecting adversary. The two halves of the body had not yet hit the floor before the Lightbringer was leaping to his friend's rescue.

But already Wolfe was trussed like a fowl for roasting. The Restrainers whirled about securing him ever tighter in their lethal embrace.

Owen elbowed his way rudely through their stately gavotte and began to slash frantically at the netting. But each time one layer parted, he found another lying beneath. And his efforts were further hampered by his having to keep on the move to avoid becoming entangled himself.

Wolfe was slowly throttling. He was gasping for air now, his face mottling horribly as the Pawns continued to bind him like an infant in swaddling clothes.

The Lightbringer analysed his dilemma. If he attacked the Pawns singly, he would not have time to dispose of them all before Wolfe's breath gave out. True, Wolfe could not die, but with his brain starved of air, he would live on as an incurable idiot. Owen must therefore subdue the single source of the Pawn's power.

He whirled towards the dais where Danu sat, an expression of vicious determination transforming her handsome face into a malevolent mask.

"Stop them!" cried the Sun-Prince.

But the Temptress ignored him.

"Stop them" Owen shouted again. "Or I will kill the Star-Child."

Whether or not he would have put this dire threat into action, Owen was never to know, for, as he leapt for the amethyst throne, an intense whine filled the Receiving Room.

Danu clapped her hands over her ears and looked up towards the source of the sound.

The Star-Child, who had remained unmoved by Owen's threat on her life, sprang from her footstool and hid behind her Guardian.

Two strides brought Owen to the dais.

As the Temptress stared upwards, eyes stretched wide in wonder at whatever was occurring at roof level, Owen brought the Sword of Infinity down onto the console, smashing it to smithereens.

The Restrainers juddered to a halt.

Owen, his head ringing from the scream of sound, which seemed to be getting louder every moment, staggered to his friend's side and cut away the restricting bonds.

But Wolfe did not even thank him. He lay on his back, staring upwards, his eyes blank with disbelief.

"The ceiling," he croaked. "Great Agador, Owen, what is it?"

Then and only then did the Lightbringer look up. The reversed Universe that had decorated the roof had disappeared in a white-hot blur. Below this spun a whirlpool of pure energy. From the vortex of this apparition issued the almost mind-bending noise.

The ball of light began to dip towards the ground. It stopped about man-height above the squared floor and imperceptibly started to slow down. And as it slowed, so the sound died away. Colours became visible. Red. Gold. White. A shape began to form. Smooth. Cylindrical.

Until they were looking at a machine. A travelling machine with a domed roof and long slits for windows. A golden machine, decorated with a central sun from which leapt scarlet flames and milk-white horses.

It hovered there on its cushion of air until it had finally stopped revolving. Then, with a sigh like pressure escaping from a pig's bladder balloon, it settled slowly to the chequered floor.

A small hatch opened in the domed roof and a young man climbed out. He shinned down the side of the machine using the toeholds that had been cut strategically into its smooth, sloping walls. Then he turned to face his astonished audience. He was approximately Owen's age. And his face was Owen's face.

In fact, the resemblance to Owen was quite remarkable. He had the same muscular build, the same aquiline nose, the same slanted cats-eyes. Only his colouring was different. His skin was golden, like the skin on Owen's right arm, and his hair, which hung half-way down his back in a rich profusion of growth, glowed a bright red-gold.

Owen had only seen such hair on one other person. His mother, Dorelia.

The young man looked about him and tentatively placed his right hand on the Sword which hung from the jewelled scabbard at his waist.

Owen looked at the Sword, then looked again. It was

identical to the Sword which he held in his own hand. It was the Sword of Infinity.

A wave of the nostalgic feeling that had hit him in the Long Barrow, washed over Owen once more. He knew this young man, even though he had never seen him. Knew him, as though he were his own . . .

"Who . . . who are you?" he stammered.

"I am Rory Firestar," announced the young man. "Son of the Lightbringer. Son of the Sun."

TEN

The Swords of Infinity

Wolfe held his head and groaned.

"This is all too much for me," he complained. "You arrive here in this outlandish machine and claim you are Owen's son. How can you be his son? You're as old as he is. Who are you really? Where are you come from anyway?"

"I think I can answer that," said Owen quietly. "He is my son. He has come from our future."

"Just so," said the red-haired youth. "This may be the first time *you've* seen *me*, Uncle Wolfe, but *I've* known *you* all my life. Why, you even helped to build this outlandish machine, as you call it." He patted the golden walls lovingly. "The Fire-Chariot. The very first Time Traveller."

"Well, you certainly arrived at an opportune moment," said Owen. "You have come for the Star-Child, I suppose?"

"Of course," nodded Rory. "As you advised me . . . or rather will advise me at some later date." He surveyed the remains of Danu's Pawns. "But it seems I should have come sooner. I've missed all the fun. Pity the co-ordinates weren't set for a few moments earlier."

"Tell me," said Owen curiously, "where did you get the co-ordinates?"

"Why, from you, Father."

"But I don't know them myself."

"Not yet perhaps, but let me assure you that when you left Tara, you had the co-ordinates with you."

"But we haven't let Tara yet," objected Wolfe.

"I know," agreed Rory. "Confusing, isn't it?"

"Tell me, Rory," said the Lightbringer, thinking it out carefully before he spoke. "In this future that you have just left, did I tell you how I came by the co-ordinates?"

"Yes," admitted his son. "But I may not reveal that to you. It is the first rule of Time travel. No-one must ever be allowed direct knowledge of his own future in case that knowledge might prompt him to try to change things. By doing so he would disrupt the balance and put everything out of sync. The results would be catastrophic."

"I hate to interrupt this reunion of strangers." Danu's sarcastic voice sliced across the conversation. "But haven't you gentlemen forgotten something? You are still in my territory. And it is still up to me whether or not you ever leave Tara. Did you think the Pawns my only weapon? If so, you are even greater fools that I had given you credit for. One battle does not win a war. It is in my power to keep you here in the Dream Palace. So I still control whatever future you have. And I predict that it will be a short one. By your meddling in my affairs, Lightbringer, you have delivered your Son into my hands. Neither you nor he shall see the Otherside again if I have any say in the matter."

Rory strode to the dais and bowed low before the Temptress of Tara.

"My apologies, Danu," he said. "I have been less than chivalrous. In my excitement at seeing the Lightbringer I had quite forgotten my manners. Please forgive me and try to understand. It is not every day a man travels through Time. Allow me to present my compliments and my humble suit. I beg that you grant me the hand of your ward, the Star-Child, in marriage."

"Do not mock me, Flaming-Hair," hissed the Temptress, "with your pretty manners and your prettier words. You shall never marry Astra. I have already told your Father my plans for her, so I will not trouble to explain them again to you. No doubt he has already advised you of the details in that future from which you claim to have come."

"Quite so," nodded Rory. "But perhaps Astra has something to say about these plans to which you propose to subject her. Where is she?"

A small, silver head wreathed in roses peeped from behind the folds of Danu's flowing gown. Two silver-fringed eyes took in the figure of the red-haired Prince. Evidently they approved what they saw for, moments later, the Star-Child stepped from her hiding-place.

Rory stared at her in stunned silence before dropping to one knee.

"My Father did you a disservice," he marvelled. "You are far more beautiful than his description."

"Rise, Sun-Prince," said the Star-Maiden with a shy smile. "Know that I also find you to my liking. And that it pleases me to accept your suit. For I consider Danu's plans — and her choice of my prospective husband — both repulsive."

She held a tiny silver hand out towards the kneeling youth.

But as Rory rose to take it, Danu slapped it aside with a scream of rage.

"Ungrateful wretch!" she screeched. "Have I housed and nurtured you all these years to see my plans come to naught at this juncture? No, viper, I am not so easily thwarted."

She whirled about, knocking the pieces of the ruined console to the far end of the dais in her fury, and stabbed at a small lighted square on the surface of the great, grey machine, which still hummed away behind the amethyst throne.

A thick curtain of transparent crystalglass swished down from the roof, slamming into the floor in front of the dais so that not a crack showed between the two.

Wolfe had a fleeting image of the central chamber in the Long Barrow of Kilken, plunging into darkness as the stone slab fell, cutting Owen and himself off from the outside world. He shuddered at the memory.

"Now," Danu's voice crackled through the sound boxes. "We shall see who controls the future."

She pulled down a scarlet lever on the side of the machine.

"Are you hungry, Astra?" she enquired solicitously. "How would you like a little roast manflesh for supper?"

In the main area of the Receiving Room, the temperature rose suddenly. Smoke started to seep from the cracks between the piebald paving-stones. The anthracite walls, which had

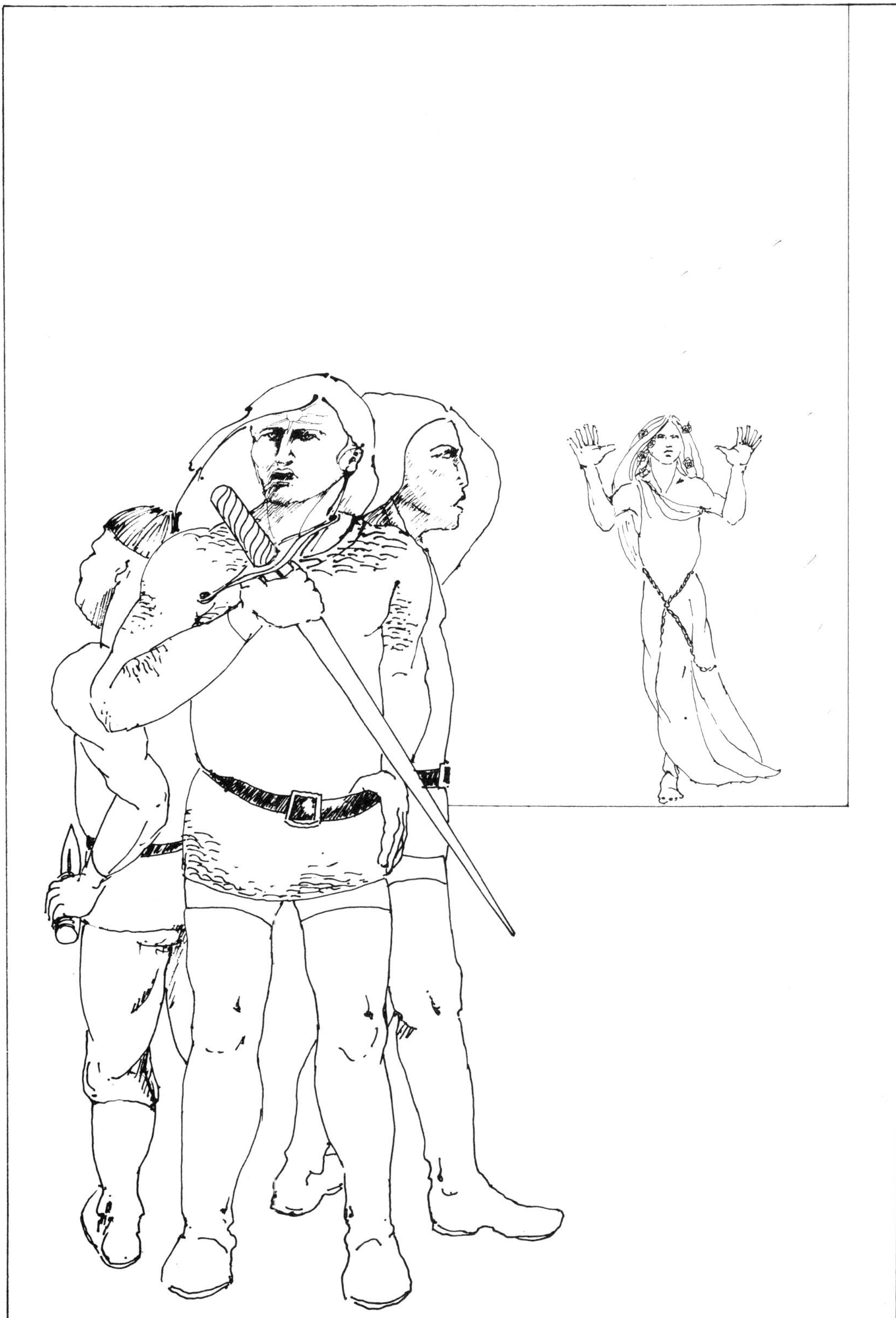

begun to radiate heat, gave a shudder that shook the Dream Palace to its foundations, and started to creep slowly inwards.

"Great Agador!" Wolfe cursed, hopping up and down as the heat started to penetrate the soles of his boots. "That vixen means to cook us alive."

Behind the crystalglass partition, Astra flung herself towards Rory, battering feverishly against the wall that separated them.

Danu's hysterical laughter swooped down from the glowing walls.

"Take a last look at your love, foolish child," she crowed. "Soon he will be no more than a burnt-out cinder."

Rory turned agitatedly to Owen.

"Father," he pleaded, "you did not tell me about this part. What do we do now? How do we save Astra from that Helligan?"

"Save her?" snorted Wolfe, eyeing the approaching walls with considerable trepidation. "Better think about saving yourself, young man. It's you who are about to be reduced to ashes."

The walls had moved to within a few paces of the Fire-Chariot. Its golden sides showed signs of blistering in the heat. All three men were now bathed in sweat, their clothes sticking to their bodies, hair plastered to their heads.

"Wolfe's right," gasped Owen, wiping the salty liquid from his stinging eyes. "Astra is safe for the moment, but we must get out of here. Can we escape in your Fire-Chariot?"

"I'm afraid not," Rory shook his head. "We are from different times. We cannot leave Tara together. It would disrupt the circle."

"Then you go," said Owen urgently. "Save yourself!"

"Useless." said Rory. "Don't you see? If you die now, I will never be born. And anyway, I could not leave you in such a predicament. My place is here, with you . . . and Astra."

"Then there's only one thing for it," said Owen grimly. "I shall have to test the might of the Sword of Infinity against the strength of Danu's crystalglass. Let's hope I can split it."

He closed his eyes and raised the great Sword to his head in a silent salute to the unseen Sun, his ancestor. The Mark that shone on his forehead, like the third eye of legend, began to throb in time with his rapidly escalating heartbeat. Adrenalin pulsed through his veins in a golden flood, embuing him with strength and courage.

Then, with the battle-cry of the Sun-Kings on his lips:

"AGADOR VANZORIBUS!"

he opened his eyes and hurtled towards the transparent screen. Focusing all his concentration on the tip of the Sword, he drove the great weapon, point foremost, into the solid partition.

With an unholy crack, it shattered into a miniature hailstorm through which Astra flung herself into Rory's waiting arms.

But the impetus of the Sword carried it and Owen on. The blade plunged straight through Danu's ample breast and into the thrumming machine behind her. The machine exploded in a shower of sparks and the white-hot walls ground to a halt.

Gingerly, Owen withdrew the Sword. As it left Danu's chest, the ectoplasm that surrounded her quivered slightly. Otherwise the blow appeared to have had no effect whatsoever.

"I have stood in the pathway of the Flame of Life!" sneered the Temptress. "Your Sword-Blade cannot harm me."

"But perhaps mine can," said Rory, drawing *his* Sword of Infinity from its scabbard. As the tip left the sheath, man and weapon became outlined in the Sacred Fire of the Sun-Kings. Now two young men stood like living flames facing the evil figure of the Enchantress of Tara.

"We have an interesting situation here," said Rory conver-

sationally. "A woman who has passed through the Flame of Life and therefore may not be killed, not even by the greatest weapon ever forged. Stalemate? Not quite. For there is something which this woman fears more than Death. She fears old age. What we see before us is not the true aspect of the Queen of the Netherworld. Too late she learned that everlasting life did not mean everlasting youth. And so she had to create an image for herself.

"So, you are nothing more than a mirage, Danu. A beautiful picture. But you are not the only mirage in this room. The Sword which I hold in my hand is also a mirage. It cannot be the real Sword of Infinity for the Lightbringer holds that. My Sword is from another Time sequence. His belongs to the Now. So my Sword also is but a picture. And perhaps a picture can destroy a picture? What do you say to that Danu?"

The Temptress took a faltering step backwards, a look of

mingled hate and fear dulling her violet eyes.

"You wouldn't dare," she snarled.

"Wouldn't I though?" smiled Rory. "You'd be surprised what I'd dare . . . for Astra . . . and for the Sun-Dynasty."

He stepped forward and, very gently, brought the second Sword of Infinity down through the Queen's body.

The curling tendrils of ectoplasm melted away and with them the voluptuous figure of the Temptress of Tara. In her place stood an old, gnarled woman, wrinkled and raddled with age. It was the hag who had foretold their futures in the Long Barrow of Kilken.

Danu lifted one shaking hand to cover her withered features. The Magic Ring of Tara slipped from her shrunken finger. A tiny circle in the Circle of Time, it rolled off the dais and came to rest at the Lightbringer's feet.

ELEVEN

The Magic Ring of Tara

Rory bent to pick up the plain, iron ring.

"Give it to me," begged the old woman, clawing desperately at the empty air. "Give me back the Ring."

But the young, red-haired Prince ignored her, handing the coveted piece of jewellery to his Father instead.

"This is what you came to Tara for," he said. "And now that you have it, I suggest you shake the dust of this place off your feet with all speed."

"We will," Owen assured him, tucking the Ring into a concealed pocket in his tunic for safekeeping. "Just as soon as we've seen you and Astra safely off."

"No, you must go first. We'll stay here and keep watch on Danu. At least until you are safely out of the Palace of Dreams. Our future depends upon it after all. You hold the Ring, without which I will never be born."

"Agador preserve us," groaned Wolfe. "Don't start all that again. I'm so confused I don't know if it's yesterday or tomorrow."

"It is both," grinned Rory. "Somewhere in the Circle of Time."

"That's as may be," grunted the Wolfeslayer. "But what

I'm interested in right now is the present— and getting out of here."

"Hee, hee, hee," tittered the Temptress, her raddled face puckering into a mass of wrinkles. "Easier said than done. Only I know the way out of Tara. And I'm not telling. Though I might be persuaded," she added craftily, "if you were to give me back the Ring."

"No need," interrupted Rory. "I, too, know the way out. My father told me the story of his adventures in Tara many times. I know them by heart. He told me how he and the Wolfeslayer escaped, and that much of his future I am empowered to reveal to him . . . to keep the Circle of Time in motion."

He turned to his Father.

"Behind the machine on the dais, you will find a secret door. Beyond it lies the Bridge of Light which spans the bottomless pit that is the very heart of Tara. Cross that Bridge and you will come to a turning wheel of fire. Do not be afraid, for like the Sacred Fire of the Sun-Kings, it will not harm you. Pass through it and you will find yourself back in your own time, on the Island of Kilken."

"There's a door here right enough," shouted Wolfe, who had leapt onto the dais and now stood peering behind one of the warped panels of the disabled machine.

"You shall not go through!" screeched Danu, flinging herself on the Wolfeslayer and battering his barrel chest with her shrunken fists. "Get away from there. I command it."

But Wolfe's only response was to wrap her sparrow's body in the folds of her, by now, ludicrously overlarge gown, and plonk her unceremoniously onto the amethyst throne.

"Now you stay there," he said sternly, as one might caution a disobedient child. "And let's not have another peep out of you. Owen, are you coming or not? The sooner I get out of this heathen place, the better I'll like it."

"I'll be right with you," said Owen, holding his golden hand out towards his Son. "Just as soon as I've said my 'Goodbyes'."

Rory ignored the proferred hand and instead threw his arms around the Lightbringer in a bearhug. When he eventually let go, Owen noticed that there were tears in the young man's eyes.

"Cheer up, Rory," he said heartily. "We shall meet again soon, shall we not?"

He bent to kiss the Star-Child lightly on the cheek.

"And take good care of Astra," he threatened. "Or you will have me to answer to. If your mother was not so beautiful I should envy you, Rory."

"Owen!" shouted Wolfe from the doorway. "In Agador's name . . ."

"Coming, coming," answered the Sun-Prince, and with a final wave, he leapt onto the dais, squeezed behind the burnt-out wreck of the great, grey machine and was gone.

The Temptress slumped down in her throne in an attitude of abject despair.

Silence settled on the Palace of Dreams.

Rory pulled a gold, silk handkerchief from his jerkin pocket, unfolded it, removed the small, metal object it concealed and then miserably blew his nose.

"Do not be so sad, my love," admonished Astra, wiping a stray tear from the corner of his eye. "As your father said, you will see each other again soon."

"No." The Sun-Prince shook his head sadly. "*He* will see *me* soon for in his time I am not yet born. But I will never see him again. In the time from which I have come, the Lightbringer is already dead. He died two days ago in a hunting accident just outside Stonehenge. He has already gone to join his ancestors in the Pyramid of Anakrion."

"Good riddance," croaked the creature on the dais. "May

his memory be forever reviled."

"You may yet mourn the dead, old ingrate," said Rory furiously. "Before he died my Father gave me two things. The Sword of Infinity . . . and this."

He held out the small object he had taken from the golden handkerchief. It was a plain, iron ring.

"He asked me to give it back. He said he knew what it was to exist under the threat of living death. He said it was a fate he could not wish on anyone. Not even you. Here take it. It is the Magic Ring of Tara."

With an inhuman squawk, Dana plucked the ring from Rory's hand and thrust it greedily onto her stick-insect finger.

Nothing happened. The Temptress looked around wildly.

"It doesn't work," she keened. "It has lost its power. It has not made me young again. It is a trick. It is some other ring. A fake. I should have known better than to trust an accursed spawn of a Sun-King."

She scrabbled the Ring off her hand and peered at its inside perimeter. There, sure enough, were the engraved runes with which the Magician-Smith Giobnhu had invested it with its magic powers so long ago. It *was* the Ring of Tara. Danu flung herself on the ground then, and began to kick and scream, an over-age infant in the grip of a collossal temper tantrum.

"I want to be young," she wailed. "I want to be beautiful. I won't be old and hideous. I won't. I can't bear it. Why doesn't it work? Why? Why?"

And she burst into floods of tears.

"It will work," said Rory quietly. "But not right away. You must preserve yourself in patience a while yet. Just as there cannot be two Swords of Infinity with the same powers in one time sequence, so there cannot be two Magic Rings of Tara. Until my Father leaves this Netherworld with the other Ring, *yours* will be no more than a useless replica. Are you so foolish as to believe that I would risk giving you the Ring of

Tara, if there was the slightest chance you might use it to prevent the Lightbringer from returning to his own universe."

He put an arm around the Star-Child's slender silver shoulders.

"And now," he said, "perhaps you would care to say a last 'Goodbye' to your guardian? We must be on our way."

Hesitantly, the Star-Child approached the amethyst throne, mounted the dais and bent to kiss Danu's wrinkled cheek. The repulsive old hag spat at her like a poisonous viper and caught her a stinging slap across the face. The iron ring left a small dark imprint on the silver skin.

"Begone Traitoress!" she hissed. "I wish now I had left you to die when you fell from the sky, rather than wasting my precious time on such as you."

"Time is all you wasted then," said Astra, biting her lip to hold back the tears. "For in all the years I lived with you, you never showed me one act of affection, or gave me one word of love."

Danu's clawed hand snaked out, clutched a handful of the soft, silver hair and yanked the girl's head down until her face was almost touching her own.

"Love? Is that what you wanted? I have offered you something much more durable. Power. Power, not only over this universe but over all universes. But you had neither the sense nor the gratitude to accept so monumental a gift. Make the most of your puny love then. For you will not have it long. Do not make the mistake of thinking you have won. I swear as I am Temptress of Tara, that I will repay your treachery a millionfold. My revenge will fall, if not on you, then on your children and your children's children, as yet unborn and unbegot . . ."

"Enough, old scorpion," said Rory sharply, unwinding the silver strands from Danu's palsied fingers and lifting the shaken Star-Child from the dais.

"Pay no heed," he reassured his bride-to-be. "Her threats are nothing more than the mouthings of a demented old woman. You must not let them upset you."

"I cannot help it," faltered Astra. "I fear her . . ."

"You must not. I am here to protect you, now . . . and always. And those universes of which she speaks, she no longer has the power to give them to you. But they shall be my wedding gift. We return now to Stonehenge, but after the marriage ceremony we will journey in the Fire Chariot back to the Stars from which you came."

Gently he led the Star-Child to the side of the Fire Chariot and, showing her the handholds cut in the golden walls, watched while she mounted to the entrance of the Time Machine. When she was safely inside he followed her, pausing briefly before closing the domed hatch to stare down on the wicked old woman who glowered back at him from the debris of her dreams.

"Goodbye, Danu," he said. "I trust we shall not meet again. But just in case we do, I warn you, be on your guard. You shall not receive the same charity from me as you have done from my father."

And he closed the lid on the great golden machine with a clang that echoed around the Receiving Room like the knell of doom.

Moments later, the hum that had heralded the Fire-Chariot's arrival, announced its departure. The machine rose from the floor and began to turn, slowly at first and then faster and faster. And as it turned, the horses and the flames that decorated the sides seemed to leap into action. The whine increased in intensity as the chariot spun ever more swiftly, the horses plunging frenziedly amongst the flickering fires. They whirled until the eye could no longer distinguish shape or form, dissolving into a mere blur of colour. When even that faded, the ball of light lifted towards the starlit ceiling.

And then, quite suddenly, it was no longer there. Sound and machine ceased to be in the same instant and Danu found herself once again alone in the wreck that had been her Receiving Room.

She removed her hands from her ears and cast her eyes across the chequered floor where the remains of her Pawn courtiers lay scattered in untidy hummocks. Her rheum-filled eyes came to rest on one complete figure. She blinked in disbelief. It was the Messenger-Pawn.

He lay, untouched by the battle, face downward in the position of obeisance he had assumed when he had introduced the two strange newcomers.

The old Queen gathered the flapping bronze gown around her wasted body and scrambled awkwardly down from her dais.

She hobbled over to her one remaining servant and kicked him savagely in the head.

"Up, sluggard," she commanded. "I have work for you to do."

But the Mechanical Man gave no sign of having heard. His metal limbs did not stir. The machine that had given him life lay in ruins beside the amethyst throne.

Cursing foully, Danu bent and scrabbled about in the Pawn's back cavity. Feeling for the appropriate wires, she activated his mechanism by hand.

Slowly, stiffly, the pale body clambered upright and bowed low before his metamorphosed mistress.

"Those upstart Princes of the Sun think they have me beaten," hissed Danu, jabbing a bony forefinger into the Pawn's unfeeling chest. "But I still have a few surprises up my sleeve."

She ground her toothless gums together in fury.

"There is still time for me to stop the Lightbringer before he leaves Tara. Stop him and kill him. In that one act, I will wipe out both Father and Son . . . and that ungrateful wretch, Astra. With the father murdered and the son unborn, she and the Fire-Chariot will cease to be . . . somewhere between now and then. They may have foiled my plans for the future, but they shall not escape my revenge."

She burst into a screech of maniacal laughter that made even the robot Pawn wince.

"I will show them," cackled Danu. "I will show them who is the Mistress of Time."

"Your orders, Danu," droned the Pawn. "What would you have me do?"

"Do?" hissed Danu. "Isn't that obvious to you, Beetle-brain? Go summon up Cernunnos from the depths. Tell him I want the Lightbringer and his miserable lackey destroyed."

TWELVE

Cernunnos Rising

Owen and Wolfe stood on the edge of the yawning chasm and stared down into its stygian depths. Here and there a small winking fire and an occasional puff of sulphurous smoke gave evidence of desultory volcanic activity. Otherwise the sheer walls sank eerily into black silence.

Behind them the revolving door had closed flush with the rock, leaving them no way back.

In front, the Bridge of Light hung over the bottomless pit like a rainbow in a storm-dark sky. Where its opposite edge touched the cavern walls, a crooked path led up to the rim of the crater. Above this, the horizon hung blood-red, as though somewhere behind that jagged lip a great city lay in flames.

Owen placed a tentative foot on the bridge. He sank ankle deep into the swirling colour. Little dots of light floated upwards towards his knee, like dust-motes dancing in a sunbeam. But the bridge held firm.

He turned and beckoned to the Wolfeslayer, who stood looking distinctly uncomfortable, on the brink of the awesome drop. To him, the bridge, rail-less and dangerously narrow, represented not the way to salvation, but the realisation of a recurrent nightmare he had had since childhood.

He stood on a great height looking down. Suddenly his foot

slipped and he was hurled into space. Then he was plummeting down. Down into everlasting blackness. Down to inevitable death.

"Come along, Wolfe," Owen urged. "We must hurry. The Wheel of Fire must be on the other side of the ridge. We have still quite a way to go and who knows what nasty surprises Danu may be planning for us?"

"I can't, Owen," groaned Wolfe, knee-joints locking tight at the thought of moving. "Ask anything of me, but don't expect me to cross that bridge."

"But you must. There *is* no other way."

"In that case you'll just have to leave me and go on by yourself. Nothing would induce me to set foot on that bridge. Nothing."

"Don't be foolish. You know I can't leave you. Come on. Make an effort. Here, take my arm. And whatever you do, don't look down."

Wolfe clutched at the Lightbringer's golden arm like a drowning man, but his feet refused to budge. They felt as though they'd been nailed to the ground. Beads of perspiration broke out on his forehead as he tried, by sheer willpower, to get his leaden limbs moving. But they ignored him and he remained firmly rooted to the spot.

Half in shame, half in despair, he squeezed his eyes tightly shut, blotting out the horrifying drop that sank away beneath his feet.

The soothing darkness brought him some relief from the irrational fear that threatened to overwhelm him. He managed to shuffle one step forward . . . then another . . . and another.

"Good, Wolfe," said Owen encouragingly. "Very good. Now, just hang on to me. Keep your eyes closed. I'll guide you across."

Slowly, step by tortuous step, the two tiny figures edged across the narrow bridge.

They had almost reached the half-way point when the huge vampire bat rose vertically out of the darkness. Its shrill, squawking cry ruptured the silence and the wind of its passing ruffled the Sun-Prince's flaxen hair. Button-bright eyes as big as saucers peered out over an ugly snub nose and, as the creature wheeled above them, yellow poison from his discoloured fangs dripped onto the Light Bridge in small hissing spatterings.

Owen judged its wing-span to be at least six times the length of a man.

He judged this by the Man-Thing that rode on its back.

It sat astride the airborne charger, cloven-footed hindquarters dangling like hairy earrings on either side of the bat's triangular head. Leathery wings were folded neatly across its broad shoulders and a long, scything tail lay coiled like a well-oiled spring over the bat's furry back.

Huge branching antlers crowned a long, narrow skull. Fierce eyes, slitted with meanness and hate, glinted over the hooked nose and cruel slash of a mouth. From the pointed ears and dilated nostrils sprang little tufts of rusty hairs.

It was Cernunnos. The Horned-One. Half man. Half beast. Lord of Darkness. Master of the Nether Regions.

He was naked but for the flaming cape that swirled around his oily body. In one horny hand he held a fiery lance. In the other, a three-pronged trident.

As beast and rider swooped low over the pair on the bridge, the Horned-God threw back his head in a bubbling snarl of demonic laughter. A cloud of evil-smelling steam hissed from the cavernous throat to engulf the two humans.

Instinctively, Owen ducked, let go of his quaking friend and reached with the golden hand for the Sword of Infinity.

The Wolfeslayer opened his eyes, looked down and was immediately overcome by giddiness. The world swam around him, full of vampire bats and strange horned beings. He sank helplessly to his hands and knees.

And then the world *was* full of bats, though these were of normal size. They rose from the depths in noisome clouds. And with them came other creatures, harder to describe. Slimy, crawling loathsome monstrosities, slithering out of nooks and creeping from crannies, oozing up and out of the rocks walls to invade the Light Bridge in a welter of claws and teeth.

Owen had faced demons before, in the Central Chamber of the Pyramid of Anakrion, but they paled in comparison with the disgusting deformities that confronted him now. They struggled upwards in ever-increasing numbers, wriggling onto the bridge from either end to trap their two victims in the centre.

The Son of the Sun took a deep breath and slid the Sword of

Infinity from its jewelled scabbard. The fire of the Sun-Kings sprang to life and he stood, a flaming jewel in the centre of the rainbow crown waiting for the first of the fiends to arrive.

At his feet quivered the Wolfeslayer, a helpless mass of inability, downed, not by cowardice, but by a vertigo which he was powerless to control.

The air pulsed with thousands of furry black bodies. Urged on by their horned Master, they rained slime and faeces down on the Lightbringer's golden head.

And then the first of the monsters slithered across his foot. Owen swung the Sword of Infinity upwards and outwards in a flaming arc that cut a deadly swathe through the ranks of the ungodly. A veritable swarm of demons and bats hurtled, with hollow cries, into the darkness that had spewed them forth.

As the next batch advanced, Owen raised the great Sword above his head and shouted aloud the battle-cry of the Sun Kings.

"AGADOR VANZORIBUS! Death to the Dark Destroyer!"

With a screech of outrage, Cernunnos drove his vampire bat straight at the Sun-Prince. But Owen began to swing the Sword around his body again. As well as despatching the demons, the circular movement protected him from direct attack.

At the last moment, the Horned-God deflected his steed to the left, catching the shivering form of the Wolfeslayer a glancing blow from his flame-lance. It was enough to turn the crouching body end-over-end over the side of the bridge.

The Wolfeslayer gave one strangled gasp as his nightmare became reality. But before he could begin his sickening descent, a golden arm shot out and grabbed him roughly by the collar.

The Lightbringer had done the only thing possible to save his friend from certain death. He had dropped the Sword of Infinity and grabbed the Wolfeslayer's jerkin in his golden fist.

Of his two arms the golden one was the one with the super-strength. Even so, the older man's weight pulled him to his knees. The golden muscles bulged with exertion as Wolfe's body jerked to a halt, dangling aimlessly over the void like a pendulum without a clock.

The demons swarmed over the two men like worms on a dog's carcass. As the filthy creatures undulated out onto the Wolfeslayer, their extra weight on Owen's arm became almost too much to bear.

"Leave me," groaned Wolfe, feeling already the heart-stopping horror of the fall, which he now knew must inevitably come. "Let me go, Owen. It's the only way you can save yourself."

"Shut up," said Owen, gritting his teeth as a particularly repulsive specimen, half-rat, half-reptile, sank its pincered jaws in his neck.

A snail with a human head and hands attempted to lift the Sword of Infinity. The great weapon gave a banshee howl and glowed suddenly white-hot. The sizzling slug-thing slid off the bridge with a glop, leaving behind a shiny trail and a stench of charred blubber.

But in truth even Owen felt it was now only a matter of time. He was weakening rapidly. Even though the Sword could not be used against him he knew that without its help he could not hope to hold off the demons *and* save his friend.

A clutch of writhing spider-frogs scuttled onto him. He sank slowly to his stomach, flailing feebly with his free hand as they tore at his flesh and sucked at his veins. He was faint now from loss of blood, dizzy and disorientated. He could feel the cloth of Wolfe's jerkin slipping from between his weakening fingers.

And then a great roar reverberated around the crater, the roar of many voices, and with it came the sound of running feet.

The bridge began to heave and sway under Owen's body. With one last monumental effort, he dragged himself into a sitting position, swatting away a scorpion-headed lizard that dangled in front of his golden eyes.

Striding across the bridge came Giobnhu, Magician-Smith of Tara. Around his white head, tinted pink by the haloing scarlet sky, flashed an enormous fiery sword. With each blow he struck, a host of demons fell screeching into the pit below.

Behind Giobnhu came a huge contingent of Dwarves, each brandishing a smaller version of the Smith's magic sword. With grim thoroughness they mopped up the monsters that their master had missed, carving the demons into unrecognisable slivers before hurling the remains into empty space.

Giobnhu strode knee-deep through the devil's brood to the Sun-Prince's side. He reached over and yanked the Wolfe-slayer from his hanging hell, seconds before Owen's cramped fingers gave out. Plonking the shocked Wolfe down, he dusted away his quota of demons like so many maggots. Then he waved his Sword under the Lightbringer's nose and grinned delightedly.

It works," he crowed. "The formula works. What you see before you is an army equipped with the equivalent of a hundred Swords of Infinity. Impressive eh?"

"Very," panted Owen. "I can't remember when I've been so impressed. But did you have to cut it so fine?"

"Ungrateful boy," roared Giobnhu. "You can thank your lucky stars that I got here at all. If it wasn't for my very efficient spy system . . ."

He broke off as the shadow of dark wings fell across his pink-stained hair.

"Giobnhu," hissed the Horned-One, hurling a bolt from his flame-lance at this age-old enemy. "The Golden One is mine."

The Smith side-stepped nimbly, bumped into the Wolfeslayer and almost sent him over the edge again.

"Ow-w-w-w-w," whimpered Wolfe, sliding to his hands and knees in a renewed attack of giddiness.

"Leave him to me, Master."

The voice was Foodhunter's. He stood at the far end of the Light Bridge clamly fitting a metal-tipped arrow into his hide-strung longbow.

"Take him then," yelled the Magician-Smith. "Your time has come, Cernunnos. The arrow has been tipped with rune-marked iron. Even you may not escape it."

With a curse, the Horned God dragged his winged steed away from the Light Bridge and flung it into a series of complicated aerial manoeuvres, each of which brought him closer to the Hunter-Dwarf and his magic arrow.

Foodhunter drew back his arrow and watched the Lord of Darkness approach.

"Don't shoot until you see the reds of their eyes," he chuckled to himself, sighting the moving target as he had sighted so much panicked game.

Finally, when the beastly pair were almost upon him, he let the arrow fly free.

But the Goat-God pulled his steed up sharply to form a living shield. The Magic arrow sang, straight and true, into the heart of the huge black bat.

Cernunnos felt the animal falter beneath his hairy haunches. Hastily he scrambled into a crouching position.

But the bat's sudden demise had caught him somewhat off-guard. He had not quite unfolded his own wings when the great beast plummeted into the chasm. The Horned-God wavered off balance in the dark air.

In that moment, Owen snatched up the Sword of Infinity and hurled it, like a flaming lance, straight at the Goat-King. The magic weapon sliced through Cernunnos' left wing and fell, with a clang, at Foodhunter's feet.

The Horned-God flapped frantically above the void, but the remaining wing alone was not enough to keep his heavy body aloft.

With a screech of mingled fear and fury, he began to nose-dive. His one good wing fluttered uselessly, his cloven hooves lashed the air, his long tail swished from side to side in search of a hold with which he might break his fall.

He found one momentarily, a protruding ledge which he grabbed with tail and claw. He hung there for a brief time. Then the weight of his huge horned head overbalanced him and dragged the scrabbling forepaws away.

He spun, out of control into the very heart of the abyss. His wail of despair could be heard long after his twisting body had disappeared from sight in the darkness.

The remaining demons began a hurried and disorderly retreat, trampling over each other in the rush to vacate the Light Bridge.

Howling with glee, Giobnhu's band of Dwarves assisted them in their exodus.

In the ensuing mêlée, Owen and Giobnhu helped the Wolfeslayer across the Bridge of Light and onto the crooked path, where Foodhunter stood leaning on his longbow with the Sword of Infinity at his feet.

THIRTEEN

Alter Ego

The Wheel of Fire leapt up before them, a burning, hollow sun.

Giobnhu and his Dwarves had left them at the top of the rise, directing them to the glowing light in the valley before heading back to the Mountains of the Moon.

"After you," said Wolfe, gallantly, bowing Owen towards the leaping flames.

"Wolfe," said the Lightbringer mockingly. "I do believe you're scared. Don't forget Giobnhu said it wouldn't hurt."

"So he did. But I didn't get to live this long by believing every fool thing I'm told."

"Then obviously there's only one thing for it," laughed Owen. "I shall just have to reassure you by example."

"Halt."

Owen froze in the act of stepping into the flaming circle.

A figure stood facing him from the other side of the Wheel of Fire.

Owen felt as though he were gazing into a mirror. For he was looking at himself. And yet there was one profound difference. It was a self that was curiously reversed. An Owen in negative.

This figure was almost entirely golden. Only the right arm,

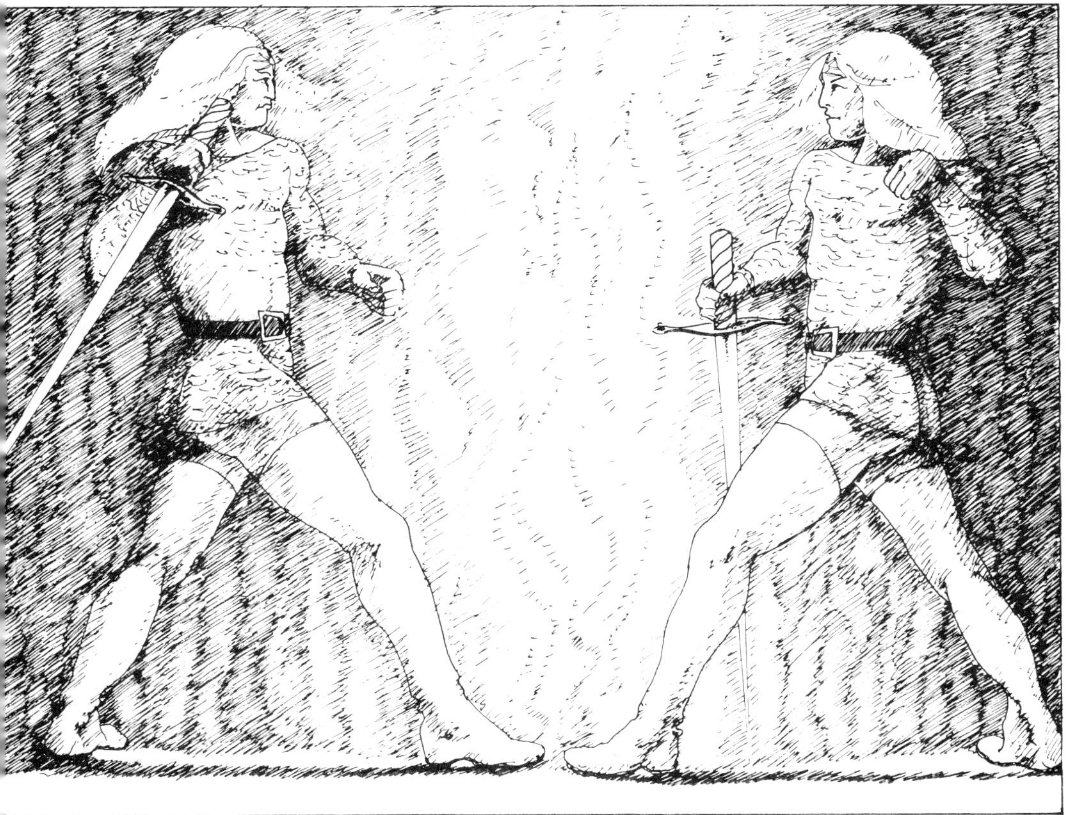

the arm which held the double-edge Sword, was flesh-coloured. That, and the Sun-Mark which stood out pale against the gleaming forehead.

There was a subtle difference in expression too. Something inherently evil lurked behind those golden features. Something which made the face, though identical to Owen's in line and form, strangely alien and repellent. The shining eyes, with their long, slit pupils, held a hint of craft.

Wolfe moved up close behind the Lightbringer and, under cover of Owen's back, slipped the killing-knife from his boot.

"By the hounds of Agador," he muttered. "Here's a remarkable thing. Who . . . or what is it?"

"I . . . I . . . don't know," faltered Owen. "If I didn't know better I'd say it was me."

The figure smiled a sinister smile.

"Right first time," it smirked. "I *am* you. Owen Lightbringer. Son of the Sun. Your other half. Your alternate face. The person you would have been had you been born in Tara. I am also the greatest enemy you will ever face. I challenge you to mortal combat. Before you leave this universe, you must overcome me . . . or be overcome."

"But you and I have no quarrel," objected the Sun-Prince. "Only a fool would fight against himself. I wish merely to return to Stonehenge in peace. Let us pass. I have no desire to fight."

"But you must . . . you must fight me . . . or remain forever in Tara . . . there is no alternative . . . I will never let you pass."

"Owen . . ."

The voice appeared to come out of nowhere.

Even so Owen heard it with profound relief. For he knew that voice. It was Xanthos, Warrior Priest of the Sun. Xanthos, who had guarded his formative years and, when he was ready, initiated him into the Mysteries. Xanthos, Wisest of the Wise, speaking to him from Stonehenge through the magic power of the All-Seeing Ring.

Owen raised his right hand and gazed into the dark blue stone.

"I hear you, Xanthos. And I welcome you. What advice do you offer to aid me in my hour of trial?"

The blue stone turned cloudy and through the white wisps the vague outline of a face appeared. It was an old face, heavy with years, steeped in authority. As the mists cleared away it began to speak.

"The one before you has been conjured up by Danu in a last desperate attempt to stop you from leaving Tara. And what he says is true . . . in part. He is indeed yourself. But he is your distaff side. He contains only your bad qualities."

"Then if I destroy him, all the evil in me will cease to exist?"

"On the contrary, you must *not* fight him. That is precisely what Danu wants."

"What then?"

"You must overcome him by power of the will. The Sword of Infinity will aid you. At some point in their lives everyone must choose the right or the wrong way. That choice is before you now. Remember what you stand for. The good and the light.

"If you fight this other self, he will win. For he will have provoked you to evil and that evil will join his evil to swallow up your good side. You will become a part of him. The evil will predominate.

"So you *cannot* lose your temper. You *must not* fight. You must face yourself. Absorb and overcome the evil that is in you. It will leave you stronger than ever before. And in your victory lies an added bonus, one which Danu has failed to take into account."

"Which is?"

"If you win you will find out. If you do not, it makes no matter. Just remember, the future of the Sun Dynasty rests on the outcome of this confrontation. Aneira awaits you . . . and so do I. Do not fail us . . ."

The voice began to fade and with it the seamed old features of the High Priest of the Sun.

"Join swords . . ." he called feebly. "Tip to tip . . ."

The mists swirled in, blotting out the ancient face. But the voice would not be silenced. Just before the stone finally solidified, it wafted weakly across time and space to deliver a last blessing.

"May your Father . . . the Sun . . . give you the strength you need to win the day . . ."

Then both voice and visage were gone and the Ring was, once more, just an elaborately fashioned piece of silver jewellery.

"On guard," cried the figure in the flame circle, lunging at the Sun-Prince before he had time to prepare.

Wolfe, who had been keeping the apparition at bay while Owen consulted with his personal oracle, parried the blow on his killing-knife. It brought him to his knees, the sword blade cutting straight through the smaller weapon to leave its owner defenceless.

Wolfe was more outraged than frightened.

"Curse you, you Heathen shade," he yelled. "That knife was given to me by my Father."

"Then let that be a lesson not to interfere in affairs which do not concern you. And just to emphasise my point, I shall now proceed to slit your cursed throat."

"Stand away from him," cried Owen, drawing the Sword of Infinity. "Your quarrel is with me."

"Then fight!" shouted his other self, slicing through Owen's jerkin and drawing a trickle of blood from the broad chest. "Fight. Fight. Fight, coward!"

But Owen would not be provoked. He did no more than defend himself as the figure in the flaming circle cut and slashed at him with demented fury.

True he kept his temper with difficulty, for the wound in his chest stung and Wolfe didn't help, standing at the sidelines yelling bloodthirsty encouragement.

And there was one very close moment when the second Owen began to insult Dorelia, the Sun-Prince's mother, who had died bearing him. The names which the evil creature called her almost goaded Owen beyond endurance. In fact he had to bite his tongue to keep calm.

But keep calm he did, awaiting his opportunity with animal cunning.

And at last it came. The golden figure began to flag. His filthy flow of insults dribbled to a halt and he fell back to take a breath.

That was when Owen stepped forward to place the tip of

the Sword of Infinity against his opponent's weapon. The two swords fused together. And Owen began to concentrate. With all his considerable strength of will, he channelled his mind to the task of absorbing the 'thing' that faced him.

The fire of the Sun-Kings, which danced around the Lightbringer and the Sword of Infinity, began to seep along the trapped blade of the 'other' Owen's sword.

He screamed, a harsh ugly sound, and struggled to free himself with the desperate thrashings of a worm on a fish-hook. But his wrigglings were useless.

Owen had sunk into a trance-like state. His strange, golden eyes had taken on the blank stare of one who has transcended the flesh to reach a higher plain of consciousness. Wolfe had only seen that look once before, during the Sacred Ceremony of the Sun at the great Temple of Stonehenge. There Owen had been invested with the accoutrements of the Sun Dynasty. The All-Seeing Ring which he wore on the index finger of his right hand and the Staff of Strength, cut from the first living tree. There he had dedicated himself to the Sun and become the Lightbringer.

Wolfe was just as fascinated now as he had been then.

The Sacred Fire had reached the pale right hand, and was curling now towards the white fingers.

As though to assist in the contest, Tara's dull purple Sun began to glow brighter above the molten plain, and the golden flames of the sacred Fire gobbled up the evil Owen's right hand.

"Let me go!" he screamed, turning on the Sun-Prince a look of such malevolent hatred that the blood in Wolfe's veins turned to ice-water.

But that look was his undoing. His eyes became hypnotically linked to those of his twin. Try as he might, he could not pull his gaze away.

The Fire inched slowly around him, devouring the golden

body, bit by bit. At last only the skull remained untouched. The fear in those doomed eyes was terrible to see. He gave one last frightened bleat before the leaping flames engulfed him entirely.

Wolfe watched, as though he, too, had been hypnotised, as the fire consumed the body. It cracked and split and shrivelled like an effigy on a funeral pyre. It shrank and curled under the terrible heat and then just before it fell apart, it disappeared, like liquid being sucked through a straw, up through the shaft of the Sword of Infinity to amalgamate with the Lightbringer's body. The two-edged sword dribbled away into the earth.

Then nothing remained. Except one man holding one sword.

Wolfe took Owen by the shoulder and shook him gently.

"Owen," he murmured. "Owen. Wake up now. It's all right. It's all over."

To his intense relief, a flicker of understanding flitted across the Lightbringer's staring eyes. He blinked, looked about him dazedly, saw the Wolfeslayer and smiled.

"Is it finished?" he asked.

"It is. And you've won."

"Well, that's a relief," said the Son of the Sun, replacing the Sword of Infinity in its jewelled scabbard.

The Fire of the Sun-Kings died away.

"Strange," said Owen, "I don't feel tired at all. In fact, I feel brand new. Why, what's the matter, Wolfe? What are you staring at me like that?"

"Because . . . because you *are* brand new," gargled the Wolfeslayer. "Something's happened to you."

Owen looked down at his hands. They seemed all right. Both the same. Both gold.

Both gold?

He pushed back his left sleeve. The arm was gold as well.

Through the slash in his jerkin his chest glowed golden too. He looked up at Wolfe.

"Am I . . .?" he began.

Wolfe nodded. "Just like the Sun-Kings in the Pyramid of Anakrion. Gold through and through!"

"Then this must be the bonus of which Xanthos spoke. I have absorbed the physical characteristics of my double too. We are one. And I have conquered the evil. I am complete now. A true Sun-King. And another thing, Wolfe. I know the co-ordinates. The ones Rory needed to find this time and place. In fact, I'm sure I know a lot of things I didn't know before. My head feels fairly stuffed with knowledge."

Gravely the Wolfeslayer knelt before the Sun-King.

"Do not kneel before me," protested the Lightbringer. "This metamorphosis does not affect our friendship in any way. I am to you as I have always been and I hope that you will continue to be as you have always been . . . my true and faithful friend."

"You need never doubt it," Wolfe avowed.

"Well then, let your first test of friendship be to step with me into that Wheel of Light."

And so, side by side, the weirdly contrasting pair walked into the heart of the flaming circle . . . and out of Tara.

FOURTEEN

Ashes to Ashes

They stood outside the Long Barrow of Kilken. At Owen's feet lay the golden filet and the fur-lined cloak which Wolfe had discarded at the very beginning of their strange adventure.

He stooped to pick them up from the damp grass. Placing the filet over the faintly etched Sun-Mark, he threw the all-enveloping garment around his shoulders, taking care to pull the cowl low over his forehead to conceal the change in his appearance.

But if Owen had changed, Kilken had not. It was as bleak and uninviting as ever. The east wind still cut like a knife. The atmosphere still stank of decay.

Mawg was waiting for them on the narrow strip of beach. He did a little jig of recognition as the two men topped the rise and began to slither down the slope.

"Well well, and is it yourselves?" he called by way of greeting. "Aren't you just in time too? I was about to push off. The Sun's nigh to dying. A few more heartbeats and it'll be dark."

"Let's go then," said Wolfe with a shudder. "The sooner I see the back of this accursed Island, the better I'll like it.

"Ah now, not so fast," said Mawg, slyly. "There's a small

matter of payment."

"You'll get that when we land at Coom."

"I'll get it now if you don't mind. Thon coracle is a thran craft to handle. It takes years of practise to stop her from keeling over. You'll get nowhere without me. And I'm not budging 'til I get what's owed me."

Wolfe grinned wolfishly.

"You'd rather we all spent the night here, would you? Perhaps when the hobgoblings start creeping out of the Netherworld you'll be in more of a hurry to leave. If we don't go, then neither do you . . ."

Mawg's knees began to knock.

"A-a-and how do you propose to stop me?" he quavered.

"Like this," shouted Wolfe, grabbing the coracle and upending it over his head. Then he ran off up the beach like an animated toadstool with Mawg hopping in pursuit.

"Come back here, both of you," ordered Owen, his voice sounding sepulchrally from the recesses of the cowl. "You're worse than a pair of children with your squabbling."

He drew a small tooled leather purse from a pocket in his fur-lined cloak, and undid the drawstring.

"How much do I owe you, Mawg?" he asked.

"Thirty deenars," said Mawg, shuffling his feet. "That was the bargain, wasn't it? A deenar for every day."

"And you have been here every day for thirty days?" asked Owen gently.

"I have that," blustered the little man, colouring slightly under his tan.

"Very well."

Owen held out a golden hand. Thirty deenars lay nestled in the palm, winking in the light from the setting sun.

Mawg's close-set eyes widened with avarice. He scuttled forward and sniffed at the money as a dog might sniff at a tree.

"Don't forget he still has five deenars of yours *and* the

jewelled gauntlet," Wolfe reminded him.

"I haven't forgotten. And neither has Mawg. Have you, Mawg?"

"What?" The little man was transfixed by the sight of the gold. He had never seen so much all at one time. "Oh . . . yes," he said vaguely. "I have them in a safe place . . . back in Coom. You'll get them soon enough."

"We'd better," growled Wolfe, "or I'll know the reason why."

"Why don't you take the money, Mawg?" asked Owen, for the little man kept reaching out and then pulling his hand away at the last moment, almost as though he were afraid the gold were a mere mirage and that if he touched his hoard, it would disappear.

Mawg peered up under the Lightbringer's cowl. The golden eyes gazed unflinchingly back from the shadowed face.

Mawg wriggled uncomfortably under that uncompromising stare. He reached out once more to take the money, hesitated, then dropped his hand to his side.

"I . . . I can't do it," he said resignedly.

"Why not?"

"Because . . . ach . . . because I lied to you, so I did . . . I haven't been here thirty days at all."

"I thought not," snorted Wolfe. "I lost all track of time in that awful place . . . but I didn't think we'd been gone as long as that."

"How long, Mawg?" enquired Owen.

"Ten . . . no five . . . two . . . oh, what's the use, this is the first night I've come to see if you were here. You only owe me one deenar."

"What's going on?" yelled Wolfe. "First he tries to cheat us by pretending we've been away longer than we were . . . now he tries to confuse us into believing we've been gone only one day. Do you take us for complete idiots? What's your game anyway?"

"No game, Wolfe," said Owen. "What Mawg says is true. We've only been away from Kilken for one and a half cycles. Time does not run with the same momentum here as in Tara."

"How do you know this?" asked a puzzled Wolfeslayer.

"A Sun-King knows much. And Time he knows best of all."

"So you knew I was lying right from the start." Mawg had the good grace to look embarrassed.

"Of course. But it makes no difference. You told the truth in the end. And for that you may keep the thirty deenars. You earned them in coming back for us at all."

Mawg grabbed the money and tipped it into his grubby pouch before Owen could change his mind.

"Glory be," he crowed. "I'm rich. Sure and isn't honesty the best policy after all? Now I can marry Mavreen."

"Mavreen?"

"My intended. She and I have been walking out . . . oh . . . it must be twenty Summers now. I must admit though, she's been getting a mite impatient lately."

"I can well imagine it," laughed Owen. "In that case you'd better keep the other five deenars too . . . as a betrothal gift."

"Where I come from," sniffed Wolfe. "We'd call that throwing good money after bad."

But Mawg could hardly contain his delight. He capered up the darkening beach whooping and cavorting. Even Wolfe had to grin at his antics.

And then the last segment of the Sun dipped below the horizon and night was upon them.

Mawg's carolling came to an abrupt halt. They could hear him, though they couldn't see him, stumbling towards them along the stony beach muttering imprecations each time his foot strayed into the icy water.

As their eyes became accustomed to the dark, the three men converged on the coracle, hefted it over the right way, launched it, scrambled aboard and pushed off into the surf.

They had only gone a few strokes from shore when the night sky was torn by an ominous rumbling from deep under the earth.

An eerie, supernatural glow began to emanate from the huge grave-mount at the pinnacle of the Island.

"Merciful Heavens," stuttered Mawg, rowing as fast as his arms would function. "What is it? What's happening?"

"Nothing good by the look of it," said Owen grimly, for the outline of the Barrow was growing brighter with each passing moment.

"Wouldn't it just be my luck now?" moaned Mawg. "To be rich for the first time in me life and to be cut down before I had a chance to enjoy it."

"Save your breath for your rowing," ordered Wolfe,

curtly. "If it wasn't for your greed we'd be long gone by now."

"Oh, bless us and save us," whimpered Mawg. "It's my fault now, is it? Sure and wasn't it yourself that mentioned hobgoblins. Whatever it is, you've wished it on yourself. And on me too. Glory be, why did I ever get involved in all this? Isn't it a judgment on me too?"

The light that shone from the burial chamber was now bright enough to light up not only the entire island but also the bleak, grey sea in which the coracle floundered like an upended eggshell.

A vaporous cloud began to form on top of the Long Barrow. Huge. Menacing. It grew and solidified into a figure. A grossly magnified figure of a goat-legged man. A horned creature with slit red eyes and one broken wing. Those eyes bored into the occupants of the coracle with a look that turned the chill northern sea to ice. Small blocks of it appeared in the water and compacted around the tiny craft holding it captive.

"Ahhhhhhhh . . . 'tis the divil himself," wailed Mawg. "Heaven preserve us, we're destroyed." And abandoning all pretence of rowing, he cast himself face downwards into the bottom of the boat.

"So you thought to evade me, Lightbringer?" The deep voice slicked like oil across the dark waters. "Foolish Prince, you shall never escape my wrath."

He lifted his arms high, his flaming cloak flashing like a dragon's breath around his obscenely powerful body.

"Oceans hear me," he commanded.

"Rise to sweep
Across the Bay
Breakers leap
Like wild wolves grey
Do not sleep 'til dawn of day
Wash this upstart Prince away."

Abruptly the sea began to heave. It slapped angrily against the side of the coracle, breaking up the miniature icebergs and making the tiny craft dance drunkenly in the turbulent swell.

Mawg, who still lay with his ear pressed to the bottom of the boat, suddenly sat bolt upright, his face whitewashed with fear.

"There's a wave coming," he yelled. "A tidal wave. A giant by the sound of it. We'll all be killed for sure."

Almost immediately the wave appeared, foaming over the horizon. It was of awesome proportions, twice as high as the island itself and flecked with debris dredged up from the sea bottom. Blacker even than the black night sky, it bore down on them like an avenging fury.

"If I wasn't a Twice-Born, I'd be feeling a bit uncomfortable right now," admitted Wolfe, as the gargantuan wall of water rushed towards them.

"I've been meaning to speak to you about that," said Owen apologetically. "Since you passed through the Flame of Life, the process has been reversed. You're as mortal as I am, I'm afraid."

"Now he tells me," complained Wolfe. "I could have wished for a different death given the choice. I've already *been* drowned once."

"Oh Mavreen . . . Mavreen," moaned Mawg. "Am I never to see those blue eyes again . . . or are they brown?"

"I should think the poor girl will be better off without you," said Wolfe sarcastically. "Courting twenty years and you don't even know the colour of her eyes."

"How can you joke?" wailed Mawg. "And us all at death's door?"

"Not if I have anything to do with it, we're not," announced the Lightbringer.

"Would you listen to the man," shrilled Mawg. "As if there was anything he could do about it. As if it wasn't bad enough to die, I have to die in the company of a pair of lunatics."

And indeed their position seemed hopeless. The great wave continued to surge towards the tiny craft while, from his vantage point on the heights, Cernunnos watched its approach with gloating satisfaction.

But his smugness was short-lived. For his adversary was no longer merely a Sun-Prince, but a true Sun-King. And the Sun-King traditionally controlled the elements.

Owen raised one golden arm and pointed towards the onrushing curtain of water.

"Peace," he cried. "I command you to be still."

And the great wave sank back into the ocean, leaving not a ripple behind.

Cernunnos gave a great roar of fury and Owen Lightbringer turned to face him across the silent bay.

"Lord of Darkness," he cried. "I had hoped it would not come to this. But you leave me no option."

Unclasping the hooded cloak he cast it aside. His tall, upright figure glowed in the freezing night like a watchman's fire.

Mawg put his hands over his face and gave one squawk before sinking down in a dead faint.

The young Sun-King drew the Sword of Infinity from its jewelled sheath and pointed it towards the huge figure atop the glowing grave-mound.

The fire of the Sun-Kings flared up around his already bright figure. He stood like a flaming torch in the midst of the dark Northern ocean and began to chant in the language of the ancients.

"ZILINTHAS VERSAT OPTERSANS
WITHENTEX MERSAT HOLDERPANS
SILENSET VOX
PRESNESET KROX
EVELES TENDREX SMOLDERANS."

A grumbling complaint, as of awakening fires deep below the earth's crust, shattered the night quiet.

The Long Barrow of Kilken began to tremble as though in the grip of an approaching earthquake. Small humps appeared in its outer skin, popping like erupting boils to spew out pus-like trickles of molten lava.

The figure of Cernunnos grew faint at the edges as he attempted to re-assume the form in which he had emerged from Tara. But the Lightbringer stopped him with a look from his flashing eyes.

"Not this time, Horned-One," he commanded, sternly. "You have chosen to challenge the might of the Sun-God. And you must face the consequences. It is time you learned that the force of good is more than a match for the force of evil, that the Light can conquer the dark."

The Goat-King raised his hands to his horned head and gave a screech of defiance.

"Never!" he screamed. "You can never destroy me. I am inviolate. Unending. Like the earth, I go on forever."

"Then return to the earth," ordered the Lightbringer. "Where you belong."

The top of the grave-mound erupted in a sheet of flame, flinging a fountain of sparks upwards.

Cernunnos was bathed in a pillar of fire.

With a final desperate cry, the huge figure sank into the fiery furnace.

His disappearance was punctuated by a series of explosions that shot long tongues of flame across the heavens. The coracle rocked unsteadily in the wash set up by the shock waves.

Then with a final deafening roar, Kilken split down the middle and subsided into the sea.

By the time Mawg came to his senses, the ocean had settled back over the sizzling lava. Only a column of steam remained to show that the graveyard Island had ever existed.

FIFTEEN

The Awakening

In a few moments it would be Sunrise. The atmosphere in the great temple at Stonehenge was charged with tension.

The waiting acolytes, forming a circle round the inner perimeter of the huge pillars, stood like silent ghosts in the light from their hand-held torches.

In the middle of the stone circle, Aneira, Fairest of the Fair, lay in a deep sleep on the central sacrificial stone. Swanbane and garlic flowers were twined in her hair. She had been covered by a richly embroidered blanket, emblazoned with the Sun emblem, to keep away the night air.

They had taken her from the underground chamber at Sunset the previous evening and had stood watch over her dreaming body throughout the long, sultry night.

It was Midsummer Night. The night of the Solstice. The timing was crucial.

As the Sun rose between the twin-forked hills, a beacon of light, charged with concentrated energy, would fall directly onto the sacrificial slab and Aneira's supine body. In that moment Owen must place the Magic Ring of Tara upon her finger.

Then two resurrections would take place simultaneously. The great Sun-God and his earth-bound daughter would be

re-born together.

The sky began to lighten beyond the sleeping mountains.

At the head of the granite slab, Xanthos, Warrior Priest of the Sun, moved his head very slightly under his heavy regalia and permitted himself a small sigh. He was an old man and it had been a long night. His joints were stiff and his head ached beneath the mitred helmet. Soon it would be over and he could rest.

He looked up at the young man who stood facing him at the other end of the stone. The light that shone from his strange glowing eyes lifted the old Priest's flagging spirits. He felt strength flow back into his tired limbs as the thin blood warmed in his cold veins.

Somewhere in the middle distance a Cock-bird began to crow.

Behind the pillars outside the temple, the press of people

turned their eyes towards the silent hills. A streak of orange filtered across the sky followed by a pale wash of lilac light.

"It comes," piped a small voice from the crowd. It was Icthar, son of Big Donal. He sat astride his father's huge, square shoulders and pointed towards the horizon. "See. The Sun is rising."

Xanthos raised a wrinkled hand to shade his watery eyes and stared shortsightedly at the brightening sky.

A tiny golden segment had appeared in the dip between the twin-forked hills.

"Make ready, Lightbringer," said the Priest. "The Time is almost come."

The Sun-King, tall and handsome in his ceremonial robes, held out his right hand, palm upwards.

The Wolfeslayer, uncomfortable but proud in his magnificent suit of beaten silver chainmail, stepped forward and, fumbling in his breast pocket, brought from it a plain iron ring.

In the East, the Sun nosed its way ever higher. No cloud obscured its progress. It would be a glorious day. A finger of light crept slowly across the barren plain towards Stonehenge.

Carefully, Xanthos turned back the coverlet that reached to Aneira's chin, exposing her body to waist level. She still wore the white gown in which she had been dressed when Owen rescued her from the Temple of Axylotan. It had been carefully laundered by Ellana, Daughter of the Innkeeper at the Sign of the Gryffon, who, in Owen's absence, had married her betrothed Banth and been elevated to the position of Lady-in-Waiting. The gown was draped in cool folds over Aneira's golden body. Her slender, elegant hands lay crossed on her breast.

Wolfe placed the Magic Ring of Tara in the Lightbringer's outstretched hand.

Then the complete orb of the Sun broke free from behind

the Mountains. The finger of light flooded through the two largest pillars to bathe Aneira's body in a golden glow.

"Now," announced Xanthos. "Now is the Time."

And Owen Lightbringer stepped to the side of his beloved and placed the Magic Iron Ring of Tara upon her finger.

Xanthos, Warrior Priest of the Sun, raised his hands in supplication and stared into the glowing face of his God.

"Great Sun," he cried. "Look down on this, your Daughter, and give her Life. In her name we dedicate that Life to you. Aneira, the Truly Golden, Fairest of the Fair.

Gently, Owen lifted the small, golden hand and placed it to his lips.

Aneira's eyelids fluttered. She opened her eyes and as she looked up into the Lightbringer's face, her lips curved in a smile.

Slowly she sat up. Her long, golden hair fell in fronds across her forehead and cascaded over her shining shoulders.

Owen knelt beside the sacrificial stone and bent his head humbly in the face of such beauty.

Outside the Temple, the waiting crowd gave a ragged cheer and surged forward. All Owen's friends were there. Friends he had helped, or who had helped him, during the course of his many adventures. Erich and the rest of the slave-workers from the Caverns of Doom, Big Donal and his entire camp, Tagon of the Trees, Zaralinda the old gypsy woman, Narwol the Sealman in his human guise, Mawg and Mavreen, Banth and Ellana, all pressed forward now to surround the young couple and offer up their congratulations.

But Owen and Aneira were oblivious to the noise and the well-wishers. They had eyes only for each other.

The Princess of the Sun reached forward and lightly stroked the Sun-Mark that still stood out faintly against the paler gold of the Lightbringer's forehead.

"I . . . I have had such a strange dream." she said.

"Forget it, my love," Owen reassured her. "It is over. You are safe now. You are Home."

Epilogue

So Owen and Aneira were married and in the fullness of time a Son was born to them. A golden child with his father's temperament and his grandmother's red-gold hair.

At his birth, a strange new star appeared in the Heavens. A Comet trailing a tail of fiery light. So they named the child Rory Firestar.

And Rory it was who fulfilled the ancient prophesy of the first Sun-King, Agador.

"We who have come from the Sun, shall return to the Stars."

Which is why the Sun-Kings no longer rule the Earth . . .

But if you look up into the night sky you may still see them. For when the Sun who begot them has gone to sleep, they shine on, shedding their brilliance on the Heavens, bringing light to a darkening world.